The Choosing

with my thanks —

Andrew

917-363-4535

rabbiandreamyers@gmail.com

The Choosing

A Rabbi's Journey from Silent Nights to High Holy Days

Rabbi Andrea Myers

Rutgers University Press

New Brunswick, New Jersey, and London

LIBRARY OF CONGRESS CATALOGING-IN-PUBLICATION DATA

Myers, Andrea, 1971—
  The choosing : a rabbi's journey from silent nights to high holy days /
Andrea Myers.
      p.   cm.
  Includes bibliographical references.
  ISBN 978-0-8135-4957-6 (pbk. : alk. paper)
  1. Myers, Andrea, 1971– 2. Lesbian rabbis—United States—
Biography. 3. Jewish converts from Christianity—United States—
Biography. 4. United States—Biography. I. Title.
  BM755.M94A3 2011
  296.6'1086643—dc22
                                                        2010021015

A British Cataloging-in-Publication record for this book is available from
the British Library.

Visit our Web site: http://rutgerspress.rutgers.edu

Manufactured in the United States of America

This work is lovingly dedicated to:

Rabbi Lisa J. Grushcow, D.Phil.
Ariella Rose Myers
Alice Emerson Myers
my family in Long Island and in Canada,
and in loving memory of Sally and Danny Bellafiore

Contents

Preface and Acknowledgments   ix
Author's Note   xiii

Prologue   1

1 Rosh Hashanah and Yom Kippur: Bird in Hand   3

2 The Secular New Year: Happy New Year   13

3 The New Year for Trees: The Lance and the Twig   19

4 The New Year for Animals: Because No One
   Is Allergic to Butterflies   39

5 Sukkot: Wild Turkey   54

6 Chanukah: Miller Light   78

7 Purim: Surprise Endings   94

8 Passover: I'll Be Home for Pesach   109

9 Lag B'Omer: The Work of the Chariot   118

10 Shavuot: Take Two Tablets   122

11 Tisha B'Av: Broken Sound   152

12 Elul: Hit-or-Mitzvah   167

13 Purim Katan: Customs and Gratuities Included   179

Preface and Acknowledgments

The Choosing explores what it means to survive, and to flourish, on your own terms. For me, this has meant leaving my Lutheran upbringing, coming out as a lesbian, converting to Judaism, and becoming a rabbi. This book contains the stories I have collected along the way, stories that reach across coasts, continents, and generations. Whether they take place in Germany or Jerusalem, the Rocky Mountains or suburban Long Island, they bear witness to what happens when cultures collide. Ultimately, though, this book is one of integration and transformation, showing how any real life-change should only make you more of who you are.

Rabbis are often depicted as sagely men whose stern features speak of lives spent learning ancient texts and timeless traditions. When I served a congregation in Colorado, the synagogue had a "rabbi room" in the basement, where they kept all the portraits of rabbis that congregants had donated, not knowing what to do with them. The synagogue leadership concluded that they didn't want the congregation's spiritual life defined by traditional stereotypes, so they put all the paintings in a room, mailed a tax-deductible receipt to each donor, and moved on. I learn the same texts as did the rabbis whose portraits are in that room; I celebrate the same holidays; I eat the same foods; I pray the same prayers. But I am in no way a sage, or an old-world stereotype captured in a synagogue painting. Instead, I am a rabbi, looking simply to do what rabbis have always done: to take particular, individual stories and relate them to universal themes.

When I first started telling these stories at rabbinic retreats and international interfaith conferences, I made two discoveries. First, I learned that my stories made people laugh across the divides of nationality, religion, gender, sexuality, and age. Second, I learned that, whenever I told these stories, people sought me out to tell me theirs, especially if the stories were about the holidays. The holidays of any culture have a rhythm all their own, and, when we listen, there is a natural resonance, recognition, and response. Listening to the stories elicited by my own is one of my greatest joys. I hear the theological ping in this world within the narratives of others. We are never alone. May these tales inspire you to share your own stories, as well.

———

There is a Jewish tradition known as the *tisch*, which entails rabbis sharing stories at their tables. I see this book as part of that centuries-old practice of communal storytelling, here organized around the cycle of the Jewish year. *The Choosing* lends itself to being read aloud. Inviting the reader to my table, I am telling my own tales to encourage others along the way, to help bring more understanding into this world, as well as a little more laughter.

The Choosing is not just about my own journey. My family has come along for the ride. They have gone above and beyond to try to be accommodating, and sometimes the results are quite unexpected and funny. The road to humor, not hell, is paved with the best intentions. While my parents may be unacquainted with the intricacies of Jewish law, no one is happier that I am a rabbi than my Sicilian Catholic mother and German Lutheran father. Just ask the traditional Jews to whom my mother keeps giving my business cards.

Love exists even in the most unlikely climes. Sometimes it takes a moment that brings you to the brink of sanity to realize how simple and unwavering a family's love can be. Other times, it takes your non-Jewish mother's public bear hug of an unsuspecting Orthodox man in appreciation for discount Judaica. For everything there is a season.

I am grateful to my family for providing much of the material for this book, along with their generosity of spirit, their common-sense values, and the secret ingredient: love. In particular, my grandmother Sally Bellafiore instilled in me a deep sense of conscience and unconditional love.

Jane Dystel, my literary agent, and the staff at Dystel and Goderich Literary Management gave me the opportunity to share these stories in a new way. I am grateful for their patience and professionalism. Beth Kressel played a pivotal role in helping this project take shape. I am also indebted to Paula Friedman, my copyeditor, for her skill; this book is much improved by her insights. I feel fortunate that the photographer David Fischer lent his considerable talent to this project. He displayed much patience and good humor over the course of a very long photo shoot for the cover of this book. Marlie Wasserman, my editor, and the team at Rutgers University Press, have my thanks for their encouragement and support. Somewhere my grandmother is smiling at the fact that her stories have found their way into an academic press.

The pluralistic community at the Academy for Jewish Religion, and my colleagues in the Association of Rabbis and Cantors, warrant special mention. Also, to my students, from whom I have learned the most, thank you for sharing part of your journeys with me.

Congregation Rodeph Sholom and its schools have nurtured me and my family for the past eight years. The clergy, staff, and congregants inspire us daily. The inimitable Julie Standig, talented poet and gifted reader, shared her insights and made this book a reality.

To the love of my life, Rabbi Lisa J. Grushcow, D.Phil., whose wisdom allows my mother to remind people daily that her daughter married a doctor: you have my heart and my thanks. Apart from being a Rhodes Scholar and one of the great Jewish minds of our time, you happen to look fantastic in a business suit. On all counts, I am grateful.

To our daughters, Ariella Rose and Alice Emerson: I am privileged to be your Ima. Your mother and I are more proud of you than you will ever know. These stories are yours. Treat them with care, and never be afraid of smallmindedness. Wherever possible, be strong, be brave, and catch the world by surprise. People are capable of so much more when they are laughing. When you are ready, you will add your voices to this narrative, and the story will continue. May God's face smile on you always. Try to smile back.

Author's Note

Biblical translations cited in this book are based on those of the New Jewish Publication Society (NJPS) Tanakh. Rabbinic translations are based on those provided in the Soncino volumes of Midrash and Talmud, and in Bialik and Ravnitsky's *Book of Legends*. The Baal Shem Tov quotation in chapter 4 can be found in *The Vision of Eden*, by Rabbi David Sears, and the Anton Nobel quotation in chapter 10 comes from David Ellenson, *After Emancipation* (Cincinnati 2004), 263–264, with permission. Liturgical translations are mine. Transliterations are based on the Library of Congress Hebrew table and the YIVO Yiddish transliteration chart, with a few exceptions due to familiar usage.

——

As this book is a memoir, the events described here are true, transmitted as I remember them. Some names and identifying details have been changed, but names of family members and public figures have remained the same.

The Choosing

Prologue

There are four "New Year" days: on the first of Nisan
is the New Year for kings and feasts; on the first of Elul
is the New Year for the Tithe of Cattle (Rabbi Eleazar
and Rabbi Shimon say: The first of Tishrei); on the first
of Tishrei is the New Year for the reckoning of the years,
for Sabbatical and Jubilee years, for the planting of
trees, and for vegetables; and the first of Shevat is the
New Year for trees (so say the School of Shammai; and
the School of Hillel say: on the fifteenth).
—Mishnah Rosh Hashanah 1:1

In the Mishnah, the earliest rabbinic
compilation dating from the end of the second century C.E.,
we learn that the Jewish calendar has not one but four "New
Year"s. Each has its own meaning. Most important, however,
is the underlying concept: there is always an opportunity to
begin anew. Or, as my grandmother would say, "God closes
a door and throws you out the window."

Everyone keeps track of time in different ways. My
mother, for example, remembers major family events based
on the untimely deaths of pop stars. She never gives an actual
year; rather, it is "the summer after Elvis died" or "two years
after John Lennon was killed." Sometimes, out of nowhere,
she says, "I can't believe Elvis has been dead fifteen years,"
as if we have all been counting the days. The loss of Michael
Jackson from the constellation of celebrities will no doubt
impact my family's timekeeping for many years to come.

Different years are associated with different events.
The stories that follow, based on the cycle of the Jewish year,
are accounts of new beginnings, of reinventing oneself and

finding oneself. They are stories of doors closing and windows opening, of family and community, of integration and transformation.

1

Rosh Hashanah and Yom Kippur

Bird in Hand

On the first of Tishrei is the New Year for the reckoning of the years, for Sabbatical and Jubilee years, for the planting of trees, and for vegetables.
—Mishnah Rosh Hashanah 1:1

There's more than one way to skin a chicken, but only one way to put the skin back on.
—Proverbs and other cautionary axioms of Sally Bellafiore, my grandmother

Chickens run very fast when they get upset or scared. I had the opportunity to see this firsthand while living in Jerusalem.

On the Friday morning between Rosh Hashanah and Yom Kippur, I decided to do my Shabbat shopping early, in an attempt to beat the crowds. The *shuk*, Jerusalem's famed open market, is especially frenetic at this time of year. It is supersaturated with visibly armed security, and with adventurous, wide-eyed tourists wandering off the beaten track. The locals weave their way among them, efficiently going about their business. I was proud to be a rookie among the regulars.

Unfortunately, my challah vendor happened to be across from the string of butchers doing the *kapparos* ritual. On the days between Rosh Hashanah and Yom Kippur, some communities take part in this practice, which is based on the biblical ceremony of the scapegoat. The traditional Torah reading on the morning of Yom Kippur describes how the scapegoat has the sins of the community transferred upon him, and is sent out into the wilderness. The adapted kapparos ritual consists of gently passing a chicken over a person's head, a hen for a woman, a rooster for a man, with the chicken thereby taking on the person's sins. Simply put, it is chicken swinging for the Jewish soul. Beneath all the feathers, the underlying message is one of new beginnings. The chicken takes your sins away, and you have the opportunity to start anew.

After the sins are transferred, the chicken is immediately slaughtered and taken home for dinner. There are variations in which the money, or the chicken, goes to charity. Either way, the chicken gets the short end of the stick and the sharp end of the knife.

I was born in Hollis, Queens, and raised on Long Island in the 1970s and 1980s. For years, I thought that chickens were born under plastic. As far as I was concerned, this was one of the few advantages of the sterile shopping environments I knew growing up. So the sight of dozens of chickens being slaughtered in an open-air market was horrifying.

It was not only the open market that was a culture shock. I had come to Jerusalem as part of a spiritual journey. Born to a Sicilian Catholic mother and a German Lutheran father, I had my religious education in our local Long Island Lutheran church. There, my history of biblical criticism started at the age of four. When my family was called up to communion, the pastor, gleaming in bright white vestments, proclaimed, "This is the body and this is the blood of Christ." "Mommy, mommy," I yelled, "Do we eat people? Are we vampires? Can I eat my brother?" I could feel her nails digging into my arms as she escorted me out.

It was to be the first of many such instances. I was frequently asked to sit outside of my religious school classes because my questions were considered disruptive. It wasn't that I was an atheist; on the contrary, I wanted to know more. When I was seven, I went to my pastor and told him I didn't know how to pray. He told me that reading the Bible is like praying. So I read the Bible. This led to more questions; I was especially interested in the soap opera quality of the books of Samuel, and very curious about the scene with the pretty lady in the bathtub whom the king watches on the roof. And, as much as the Hebrew Bible (which I knew as the Old Testament) was full of human foibles, it also taught me about a God who needed human beings. This spoke to me, and so I started asking questions about theology, as well. As a teenager, I finally asked one question too many, and, as a result I left the church. Not long after, I decided to leave town.

In my desperation to leave home for college, I applied to fourteen schools. When the thin pile of acceptance letters arrived, I narrowed my decision to two choices: Barnard or Brandeis. It was more than a choice between schools. My boyfriend and I were on the fast track to marriage and a conventional happily-ever-after. I had been introduced to Dennis by mutual friends, concerned about my lack of interest in men, and his lack of interest in women. Two quiet nerds, we seemed like a good fit, and by the time I applied to college, we had been together for over a year. The only catch was that I had been dating girls from the age of fifteen, and had been secretly in love with my best friend for six years. Dennis knew nothing of this; "If you stay, we should think about marriage," he said. I sent in the Brandeis forms the next day.

I had discovered Brandeis while leafing through every entry in the telephone-book-sized *Barron's Guide to Colleges*. In addition to distance, Brandeis offered everything I needed: a good pre-med program and a castle on campus. I didn't even know that Brandeis was a Jewish-sponsored university. To the best of my guidance counselor's knowledge, no one from my high school had ever gone there. The only clue, looking back, was a comment from another student. When I mentioned Brandeis, she whispered, "It's full of JAPs." I had no idea what a JAP was. Having very few Jews at my high school, I thought she meant Japanese people. I told her that I had no idea what her problem was, especially since she herself was Chinese. Her blank stare back should have clued me in.

College life in Boston was the perfect petri dish for my searching soul. Good gay clubs, lax ID checks, and over a million college students in the local area were exactly what I needed. Most important, it was too far away for my parents to visit unannounced. This bought me time to hide my Queer Nation posters, Doc Marten boots, and annoyed girlfriend. Over the years, I have had people tell me that Brandeis made me Jewish and gay. In retrospect, my odds at Barnard would have been the same. I was one of the first people from my family to attend college, and I was a young gay sponge on a spiritual search. Something was bound to happen.

My initial exposure to Jewish life at Brandeis was not promising. In my first semester there, I was having lunch with another student in the cafeteria. "What denomination are you?" he asked. "Protestant," I replied. "Oh, is that Reform?" "I guess so." Then he asked me what I was doing for the holidays. "I'm going home for Christmas," I said. He stood up and walked away, every bad stereotype he'd ever heard about Reform Judaism being inadvertently confirmed. It was my first unintentional foray into Jewish life, and my last into dating men.

It was at Brandeis that I met friends who exposed me to the joys of Jewish life for the first time. One of them took me to a *sukkah*, and it was the most fun I had ever had doing anything religious. On a more profound level, I identified with the *etrog*, the strange citrus fruit used as part of the holiday observance. Misshapen yet essential, it is an incredibly unlikely ritual object—and it carries seeds of tremendous potential. Seeing that etrog was my first inkling that I might have something to contribute to the Jewish world I was exploring. Every time I hold an etrog now, as a rabbi, I think about the moment I saw one for the first time.

I started going to Shabbat services, and fell in love with a religion that focused on questions, not answers. Simultaneously, taking pre-med classes, I realized that I could never be a doctor, an ambition that had been my operating assumption from an early age. Not only was I regularly burning off people's eyebrows in lab class, but a summer internship at a hospital in the Bronx working with people with HIV convinced me that I lacked the internal fortitude to lose patients on a regular basis. I had the heart, but I lacked the brains and the stomach. I still wanted to help people, but I wanted to be there for them in good times, as well. And so I began to imagine a different life of service—a life full of services, actually. I decided to become a rabbi.

The anachronism of that realization brought me to the conclusion that first, I had to be Jewish. I explored a Conservative conversion while still at Brandeis, but I decided to study in Israel instead. I wanted to see Judaism firsthand and really understand the nature of a people thousands of years old; I needed Israel to become part of who I was. So, after my graduation from Brandeis, I bought the biggest duffel bag I could find, got on the plane to Tel Aviv, and made my way to Jerusalem. I was a stranger in a strange land. In my first two weeks, I was pick-pocketed twice. It would have been easy to go home with my tail between my legs, but instead I never looked back. Over the two years I spent there, I felt privileged to know every street, every shopkeeper, and every free bathroom in Jerusalem.

The falafel shops hid their condiments when they saw me coming. Food also gave me the opportunity to practice my Hebrew. The first time I walked into a falafel shop, I looked at the man behind the counter and said, "*Vayehi falafel*"—a biblical phraseology borrowed from my studies of Genesis, best translated as "and there was falafel." He looked at me and smiled. His English was just as bad as my Hebrew, but good enough to correct me. Amused, he replied, "We have not asked for falafel in that way in five thousand years."

He was right, of course. And yet Jerusalem itself was timeless. I loved how, if I sat in the right coffee shop at the right time of day, I could see clerics walking by who looked like cast members from the *Lord of the Rings*. Each in their own time capsule, they would stride by like God's superheroes, while I drank my Turkish coffee and overheard the American tourists at the next table arguing about politics and religion.

When I began learning in a yeshiva in Jerusalem, I read the Talmud in English straight through because I wanted to know how it would end. Suffice it to say, I was disappointed in the lack of plot, but I was drawn in by the twists and turns of the rabbinic conversation. I joined the volunteer police and learned how to shoot a gun. I cleaned houses to make money and rationed myself to one pita, crammed with falafel and condiments, a day. I found rabbis who taught me what I needed to know about Jewish texts and traditions, and generous friends who taught me to cook and live a Jewish life. And by the end of those two years, I converted to Judaism. Ultimately, this was a journey of transformation, but also of integration. Any real life change, I learned, should only make you more of who you are.

To many, the different aspects of my identity seem like contradictions. But to me, they form an integrated whole. There is no way I would be Jewish if I were not gay, if I did not understand what it means to be hated for what you are and proud at the same time, to belong to a people as old as the world and to have a community wherever you go. Coming out gave me the ability to embrace my own path and accompany others on their travels. Converting did so, as well.

The day I encountered the chickens in the shuk, however, I was still at the beginning of my journey. I was navigating Israeli society and simply trying to find my way around. When I first moved to Jerusalem, I learned that the Hebrew word for "grocery" is *makolet*. As it happens, the word for "bomb shelter" is *miklat*. In Hebrew, these words are almost identical, and so I spent hours following the small painted signs on the buildings in my neighborhood finding shelters instead of food. As an anxious American, I was grateful for the opportunity to reassure my normally stoic mother that I knew where to find every bomb shelter within a ten-block radius of my apartment. Even more reassuring was the fact that she was concerned. This is the woman who, when I twisted my ankle in one of the holes which riddled our backyard, insisted that it must not be broken because I had no health insurance. It was strangely comforting to hear her worry from across the ocean in a way that she rarely had when I lived under her roof.

In this pre-Internet era, everything my mother knew about the Middle East was gleaned from urgent news alerts that punctuated the Motown music playing on her favorite radio station. My father's major sources were the alarmist headlines of the New York papers that he read on the commuter train to work. It was the mid-1990s; every day seemed to bring reports of new suicide bombings in Israel, and my parents were convinced that the end was near—at least for me. While they took comfort in the fact that I had established possible places of refuge from the imminent flaming apocalypse, I still needed somewhere to shop.

Once I did find my way to the shuk, I fell in love with the bounty of fresh fruits and vegetables, the olives that vendors foisted upon passers-by, and the fragrant mounds of spices. It was so different from the big-box suburban supermarkets of my childhood, with their shelves upon shelves of interchangeable brands. Here, each merchant was proud of his own small stand, and worked to make it beautiful in hopes of attracting customers. The vendors who sold challah did the briskest business of all.

Like wine and candles, challah is essential to the celebration of Shabbat. Its significance is derived from the biblical manna: two portions—or, in the case of challah, two loaves—are required. Since bread doesn't fall from heaven anymore, even in Jerusalem, everyone becomes very attached to a particular source. My personal favorite vendor also happened to be one of the most popular in Jerusalem, and the line snaked around the tightly packed passageways of the shuk. Time spent waiting on this endless line was punctuated by the din of the market and the buzzing of bees. The optimistic insects hovered over the piles of round holiday bread that sagged under the weight of heavy glazes of sweet honey and shiny egg.

As I got closer to the front of the line, the sounds of the kapparos ritual grew louder and more disturbing: a chattering chicken would be grabbed and swung, a prayer would be said, and the chicken's head would be swiftly separated from its body with the thud of a knife.

All of a sudden, something interrupted the routine. I heard a terrible shrieking squawk. It was the kind of blood-curdling, primal cry that made everyone instinctively stop and look to see where the commotion was coming from. A large rooster had broken loose, and it began running. Right toward me.

In an instant, our eyes met. The chicken swerved toward me in a last-ditch attempt to escape its sealed fate. Luck and gravity bounced the bird my way. Without missing a beat, I snatched it and tucked it under my arm. Everything turned into a grainy 1970s TV sports clip and I channeled Franco Harris's Immaculate Reception. It was the last play of this chicken's game, and I certainly was not the intended receiver. I ran toward the main road, chased by two angry men with knives, and some poor guy whose sins were still on the rooster's head. After pushing my way through the crowd, I jumped on the first bus I saw, just as the doors were about to close. The bus was filled to the rafters with Israelis, and none were pleased to see an American with a live chicken. Not an easily surprised people, however, their conversations resumed almost immediately once I made my way to the back of the bus. My new travel companion was quiet, apart from the occasional "bok" of satisfaction. He seemed to have a look of relief on his face as we pulled away from the shuk.

It occurred to me, as I caught my breath, that I had committed some kind of crime. The prospect of being prosecuted for Grand Theft Poultry worried me less than the question of what to do with this chicken. Taking it home was not an option. I cleaned other people's houses to fund my tuition, bus fare, and rent. Bird seed, ear plugs, and bleach were not in the budget. It was time for Plan B.

The last stop on the bus route was a kibbutz with olive orchards that I had begun to visit on Shabbat walks. Hoping this would be a better destination than the one where the chicken had been headed, we got off the bus. Together, we walked to the groves. I gave the chicken the stale pita bread I had carried in my pocket for a snack, and I made a basin of water with the leftover sandwich bag and the contents of my small water bottle. Only then did I realize that I had missed my chance to buy food for Shabbat, and as a result, I would be living off of ketchup packets until Saturday night. New to Jerusalem, I had an empty kitchen and no relatives or friends. I left the rooster near a thirty-foot metal sculpture of columns topped with three living olive trees, with the hope that he would make it through his first night of freedom. He, like me, was searching for a way to survive:

to make his own mistakes and to live on his own terms. As the sun went down, I turned to say goodbye. He looked up from his meal for a moment, then went back to pecking at the crumbs. I smiled. It was not quite the scapegoat's wilderness, but it would have to do.

2

The Secular
New Year

Happy New Year

On the first of Nisan is the New Year for kings and
feasts.   —Mishnah Rosh Hashanah 1:1

Make the old new, and the new holy.
                    —Rav Avraham Yitzchak Ha-Cohen Kook,
                                    First Chief Rabbi of Israel

I Left My Heart on Long Island

It happened at midnight. Piercing lights, clanging
metal, the acrid smell of gunpowder, and deafening screams
woke me out of a sound sleep. Having just returned to
America after two turbulent years in Israel, I quickly concluded that it was a bombing. A sickening synesthesia overwhelmed me, like the moment in which the senses of sound
and sight were combined in the revelation at Mount Sinai.
I saw the noise and heard the flashes of light. A burning sen-
sation coiled around my left arm and burst through my
chest like an electric shock.

There was only one other time in my life I had been so
shocked by a sound. When I was fifteen years old, my parents took me and my brother on a cruise to Bermuda. I had
a horrific period, and a friend had given me my first tampon
so that I would be able to swim. Unfortunately, I didn't
read the directions. Reader, I flushed it. Leave it to Tampax

to create a weapon so devious that it induced frenzy among the temporary residents of the *Homeric* worthy of *The Poseidon Adventure*. As the force of the ship bore down on the tiny plastic cylinder, a deafening sonic boom issued forth from the tea-cup-size bathroom. In addition to having that not-so-fresh feeling, I had discovered a portal to hell—and a way to get the attention of everyone on deck. For the rest of the cruise, I could not make eye contact with anyone. When I entered the dining room that evening, a hush fell over the room. My brother was still shaken from an orgy he witnessed on the top deck earlier that day, involving two women, a man, and a diving board: he was angry that I had upstaged him. Our vacations were nothing if not educational.

But this time, back in America, there was no wayward tampon on a cruise ship to explain the deafening sound. I tried to orient myself. Exhausted, I had walked miles to synagogue and back that evening for Rosh Hashanah, and needed a good night's rest before making the same trek in the morning. After four years at Brandeis and two years in Jerusalem, I had moved back home, penniless, to work my way through rabbinical school. My parents lived in one of the few parts of Long Island miles away from anything remotely Jewish, which made sense, given that they were not Jewish themselves. And so, on my first Rosh Hashanah back in the United States, instead of being surrounded by the festivity of the holiday in Jerusalem, I had walked alone to a suburban synagogue, sat through an endlessly long service, then walked home late at night in the dark. Now here I was, experiencing a classic Jewish nightmare come to life: being attacked in one's own home in the midst of a holiday, in the middle of the night.

The next moment, though, I realized: why would an anti-Semite attack a house with only one Jew? Perhaps this was another kind of assault. I worried about my family, my parents and younger brother in nearby bedrooms and my elderly grandmother who lived upstairs, and who was surely too frail to survive such an onslaught. Maybe this was a simple robbery gone wrong. In the years of my absence, my mother had accumulated an extensive and expensive Beanie Baby collection. Was this the thieves' true target?

All these possibilities were eliminated in one moment of clarity. The tallest of my assailants was wearing a purple sequined hat, as gaudy as one could imagine. No one would wear a hat like that but my father. The shortest of the invaders was hunched over, in no shape for breaking and entering. I recognized my grandmother's diminutive form. And with these realizations, the shouting became discernible: it was the voice of my family members, yelling "Happy New Year!" The metallic noise was the clanging of pots and pans, and the smoky smell emanated from small paper firecrackers in the shape of champagne bottles, with streamers exploding above my bed. All the members of my family were standing proudly around me, reenacting their standard ritual for the secular New Year.

My family was known for going all out on holidays; we were the ones at the end of the block whose noise permeated the neighborhood, and this was a great source of pride. In our house, everything was always on hand for a celebration. Our basement contained a series of white boxes overflowing with holiday accessories. There were boxes for New Year's, Christmas, Easter, Halloween, and Thanksgiving. No post-holiday sale was safe, and no paraphernalia too tacky, to festoon our home and its inhabitants. Out of their love for me, my parents had unleashed the stockpile in the New Year's box three months early, for Rosh Hashanah. The date and location were the only disparities from their usual celebration. Instead of the revelries spilling over from our entire front lawn into the street, my small bedroom was the focal point for the festivities.

I spent the rest of the night with the lights on, not only because Jewish law kept me from turning them off, but because I was afraid of another surprise attack. I have never liked surprises. Years later, when I was pregnant, my partner Lisa was volunteering at a homeless shelter for the night. Her shift was done early, and so she hurried home to surprise me. She tiptoed into the bedroom, blissfully unaware that, rather than snuggling under the sheets, I was standing behind the door with a baseball bat, waiting to catch the intruder.

Touched by a *Shiksa*

My family, with all their good intentions, had neglected to realize that the Jewish New Year, unlike the secular one, does not begin at midnight, and does not involve firecrackers and shiny hats. The shofar is meant to be a wake-up call, but it wakes us up for reflection and repentance, not for a party. Like the black-bean matzah ball soup my mother would make the next day, this was a cultural fusion that left a confusing taste in the mouth.

My mother realized she had not gotten Rosh Hashanah right. Wanting to make it up to me, she decided to buy me all the books I needed for rabbinical school, which I was beginning that fall. I ordered them from a Judaica store on Long Island. She drove me there and paid the nice man behind the register, and his associates helped to bring eight boxes to the car. My mother went inside to thank him. She can be an effusive woman, and words could not fully express her gratitude; totally unaware of the traditional Jewish prohibition against men and women touching, she reached toward him to give him a hug. Entering the store, I saw the man backing toward the wall, my mother on an unstoppable trajectory. The other Orthodox men lunged for their colleague; I lunged for my mother. None of us were in time. She gave him a big body hug, a full-body press like Shaq, two bricks shy of a lap dance. It was not short. The whole time, he was paralyzed, like a statue of a person from Pompeii, or like Lot's wife, frozen in salt by the horror of seeing what she should not have. My mother's eyes may have recalled an episode of *Touched by an Angel*, but the look in the men's eyes seemed to suggest "Touched by a *Shiksa*."

As I walked to the car with my mother, she asked, "Why didn't he hug me back?" "Oh, don't mind him," I replied, channeling Lily Tomlin, "he's just shy." She accepted this, even though she knew differently. It was then that I realized that my education was going to involve my whole family, and that this was a new year for us all.

Shiny Purple Hats

That first Rosh Hashanah was not the last time my father appeared at a Jewish event in a shiny purple hat. As my parents became more involved with, and aware of, my Jewish life, they retained their own sense of style. Years later, when my family found out that I was leading my first service as a student rabbi, they decided to show up en masse at the temple where I was an intern. They all came early and sat alone in the front row in their Sunday best, waiting for the service to begin, as the synagogue regulars ambled in wearing sneakers and jeans. When my part was done, they clapped. My father somehow found the most ostentatious *kippah* in the box outside the sanctuary, a resident of the undisturbed bottom strata, the relic of a bar mitzvah celebrated decades before. It was as shiny and purple as that sequined New Year's party hat. He was already the tallest one in the room, and the kippah, perched on top of his head, only added to his prominence. He folded it into his pocket when he left, and it would reemerge at many future events. The fact that he had his own personal

Jewish accessory meant that he truly was integrating it into his life.

I had come back to my parents' home thinking I could maintain a sacrosanct Jewish space, in which I could keep my own practices and customs. What I learned, that Rosh Hashanah, and in all the years that followed, was that the boundaries would be much more permeable. Although the house was not a small one, my family had a limited concept of personal space, both ideological and physical. Even the cat, Miller, would drop through the ceiling tiles from the main floor into my basement abode. My only warning would be a tapping sound on the tiles, and the next thing I knew he would be free-falling onto my couch like a fat, unwanted spider. Undaunted, he would stand up, shake himself off, and start to look for food and toys. At least, when my family descended that Rosh Hashanah night, they brought their own entertainment.

3

The New Year
for Trees

The Lance
and the Twig

The first of Shevat is the New Year for trees (so say the
School of Shammai; and the School of Hillel say: on
the fifteenth). —Mishnah Rosh Hashanah 1:1

Rabbi Shimon said: There is not one herb without its
own constellation in heaven, which slaps it and says,
"Grow!" —Midrash Genesis Rabbah 10:6

The Lance and the Twig:
Expect the Unexpected

It was a classic lesbian moment. My partner Lisa and
I were sitting in our Brooklyn apartment, playing Scrabble
over herbal tea, as our two cats rubbed against our legs. I
pushed my chair back from the table and looked her in the
eye. "I'll show you mine if you show me yours." Five minutes later, we came back to the table, each holding our high
school yearbooks.

Mine was called *The Lance*; Lisa's was *The Twig*. *The
Lance*, in title at least, followed the martial theme set by my
high school football team, the Gladiators, and the dance
team, the Romanettes, all of which was as close as we came
to the formal study of antiquity. Academics took second place
to sports. There was a math club, and I was part of it, but we

called ourselves the Mathletes ("the jocks of mathematics" was the yearbook's moniker) and tried to look tough in our photo, just a few pages away from the Rifle Club. But the truth was, the cheerleaders were tougher.

Most of all, the name *The Lance* suggested significant height and girth, something at its peak: this was as big as it was going to get. For me and my classmates, growing up on Long Island, high school was meant to be the height of life. It would initiate us into the suburban lifestyle that was portrayed as being the best of all possible worlds. The expectation was that, after high school, we would move into our parents' lives: we would buy houses in the same neighborhoods and work the same jobs. There was an implicit promise that we would work hard and receive a reward, and the reward would be a replication of the paths our parents had followed. However high our college aspirations may have been, we were always expected to come home.

It never occurred to anyone that we would not be able to afford the houses our parents lived in, or even the taxes on those homes. The peak in greatness suggested by *The Lance* would come true, but more so than anyone expected. The 1980s were a bubble in time. For many of us, the high school years really were the best years of our lives. In the shadow of a broken economy, the classmates who stayed on Long Island have moved farther east to find affordable housing. The hair has gotten smaller, and so have the dreams.

Lisa's yearbook, on the other hand, promised a beginning: great growth was both expected and achieved. She attended a prep school in Toronto for high achievers, where many students were immigrants or the children of immigrants, imbued with a sense of responsibility to go further than the generations before. The school clubs included Enviropeace and Amnesty International, and the centerpiece of the freshman curriculum was a class called the Romance of Antiquity, in preparation for studying Latin. Lisa studied Aristotle with a teacher who was genuinely Greek, and she has memories of hearing *Beowulf* read aloud in Old English in a darkened classroom. Her yearbook was full of references to academic achievement, and under the seniors' pictures were glory quotes from Nietzsche for the boys, and Indigo Girls for all the dykes-in-waiting. The yearbook's very title, *The Twig*, was based on the motto of the school, *velut arbor ita ramos*—as the tree grows, so grows the branch. This was a reference to the high school's connection with the University of Toronto, whose motto and crest featured a tree. The tree has borne fruit: the school boasts two Nobel laureates and twenty Rhodes Scholars—one of whom I married.

The most striking visual aspect of my yearbook was the hair. This was suburban Long Island in the 1980s. If you look closely at the headshots, you can see that almost all the girls' faces look smaller than the boys', because the photographer had to zoom out to include all their hair. The senior class photo bears an uncanny resemblance to a group of poodles in acid-wash jeans. To be fair, I was the photo editor of the yearbook, and so was in charge of choosing its photos. The girls I had crushes on are featured frequently, shown in their best light on prime pages. Those whom I did not like appeared in poses, and situations, that were less than flattering. The Yearbook Committee was the nerds' final revenge: the posterity of the members of our class would be decided by the people who, over the course of middle school and high school, had been abused for six years.

Over those six years, I can count on the fingers of one hand the number of times I went to the bathroom at school. In my high school, as in many others across Long Island in the mid-1980s, Camaros, football players, and big-haired girls freely roamed the countryside. Hogwarts, this was not: Harry Potter would have been killed on the spot for being a fag. My friends and I gladly risked kidney failure rather than be accosted by the menacing girls who had designated the school bathrooms as their personal space. These particular bullies wore white leather fringed jackets and dressed like jailbait heavy metal groupies; their bathroom lair was redolent of stale smoke, cheap perfume, and improperly flushed feminine hygiene products. Even walking in would be enough to induce a panic attack.

Our tenth-grade art class was held on the first floor of the school, across from a girls' bathroom. This class was ruled by a stern woman with a bun of hair tied back so tightly that it was more of a cosmetic surgery procedure than a hairstyle. She resembled a love child of the Borg Queen and Ming the Merciless. She was smart, and obviously far too talented for this venue. When she spoke of installations, we all wondered why she wanted to put her art in hardware stores.

One afternoon while I was in art class, one of the bathroom's leather-clad inhabitants made a critical error. To quote the yearbook, "Stocks in hair styling products skyrocketed as they became more widely used," and this young woman was following the trend. While applying copious amounts of Aqua-Net to her frosted dome of hair, she lit a cigarette. The hairspray ignited immediately, and so did her hair and eyebrows. Sadly, the frosting was not fire repellent. She threw the can of Aqua-Net, still on fire, into the garbage. I don't remember which came first, the screaming figure running down the hall, or the deafening blast. But despite the screams, the flames, and the scent of burning hair, our teacher's bun never moved.

I also had a problem with being flaming, albeit in a slightly less obvious, but equally dangerous, way. I had enough queer traits. I was the sole feminine presence in my industrial arts class, not including two boys who were major closet cases and whose masculinity depended on every hammered nail. My parents were uncomfortable with my decision to take the class, and my guidance counselor expressed his concerns. I replied that I could read a box of cake mix and learn how to bake, but I didn't see my father taking out power tools and showing me how to fix a lamp any time soon. So I endured the harassment—just long enough to be the proud creator of a wooden napkin holder that turned out to be more putty than wood, a malformed sheet-metal toolbox, and a lamp with stripped wires, with which I almost electrocuted my father.

I had slightly more affinity for science. All the same, it was not a particularly good idea to give a fifteen-year-old a scalpel and a lamb's heart. Or for that matter, to give three lab partners a vial of perky fruit flies, a stereoscopic dissecting microscope, a large can of ethyl ether, and a closed room. Two girls with promising futures in science and I were put in a small room with no ventilation. Since we shared the fruit flies' short attention spans we quickly decided, as soon as the teacher left, to put the ether to better use. In our infinite chemical wisdom, we decided that it was ether that, if inhaled quickly and sharply, would give one a high voice. High, we got. Though strangely mute.

We giggled and passed out. Thanks to my height and heft, the door swung open when I fell over, ventilating the room. We eventually woke up covered in fruit flies and shame, and made our way back to the classroom.

My adventures in science, however, paled next to those of the child prodigy who decided to decapitate his dissected cat and put the staring head in the faculty microwave. The English teachers ran screaming from the lounge. Whatever they were saying, it wasn't a quote from Beowulf.

The subtitle of *The Lance* in my senior year was "Expect the Unexpected." The year was defined by such surprises as a new color of lockers (blue) and a new schedule (six marking periods changed to four). As I imagined my life beyond high school, I wondered whether I could expect more.

I had an intimation of what unexpected paths I might take, at the young age of fifteen. I was auditing a college-level chemistry class, and, when I heard there was a college fair during my lunch break, I decided to go and expand my horizons. Colleges in my area liked to identify kids who were good at sports, and so it was not surprising that one college brought members of their basketball team to the fair, hoping to find new recruits. Not being athletic, however, I was completely surprised when I was approached by a tall, beautiful, androgynous-looking, Russian-speaking woman, who wrote her number on a piece of paper and told me to call her for more information. I called. We went out on a school night; I made an excuse to my parents and met her for dinner at Applebee's after school. She asked if I was interested in playing on her team.

Only later did it occur to me that she was not talking about my nonexistent athletic prowess. After dinner, she suggested we go for a walk. Suddenly I realized that there was another option for post-dinner activities, beyond television and homework. Then she opened another option: she kissed me—once on each cheek, which I understood was a European custom—and then on the lips. Now *this* was unexpected. It was a small, silly encounter but it opened my whole world. I felt like the frog in the fairy tale, transformed by a kiss. I also felt as if I had just kissed away my dreams of an easy life. In that moment, I realized how much of the world I had yet to see—and that, even if I wanted to stay home, I would have to go away.

Travels and Travails: The Tree of Knowledge

Lisa and I also had radically different experiences of travel: in particular, of family vacations. Lisa's parents took her and her brother to exotic, edifying locales like an eco-lodge in Costa Rica and an educational cruise of the Galapagos Islands. When they took her on a train trip across Canada at the age of seven, they gave her a diary so she could record her adventures. They also went on camping trips, which family photos show included sitting in folding chairs in the woods and reading books.

In my family, we visited the Amish. For nine years in a row, we took summer trips to Pennsylvania to see them in their natural environment. My mother would drive us to local farms and ask to be shown around. The women would go to the kitchen and look at the hens outside; the men would make small talk about farm tools. One summer, my mother went so far as to try to rent an Amish person from a local farmstand, hoping to secure his services and get the inside story on Amish living. The values that my mother seemed to glean from this experience were the lack of air conditioning and of cable—two things she became very proud of not having at home. Whenever we asked about the absence of anything modern or electric, the answer would be "The Amish do just fine without it."

Cable became known to me and my brother as "the fancy channels," to which we had access only at friends' houses. One night at a neighbor's, we caught a glimpse of an MTV special premiering a risqué version of "Girls on Film" with Duran Duran. I was transfixed by the sight of so many feminine men, running around with big hair. It gave me an inkling that, if only I were older and lived somewhere else, it would be a good time to be gay.

We also got tastes of air conditioning, ironically enough, during those Pennsylvania vacations. Every year, we would stay at the same blissfully cool Sheraton and eat at every all-you-can-eat smorgasbord, in cavernous rooms full of white people looking like larvae. I was reminded of these smorgasbords years later while spending a long weekend with Lisa at an inn in New Hampshire. The state's landmark attraction, a rock formation called the Man of the Mountain, had been effaced by a landslide, and we were desperate to find

something to do. Hart's Turkey Farm sounded intriguing—
to me, at least: I was convinced, given the name, that there
would be turkeys. Lisa was more skeptical. We drove for an
hour, only to find a cavernous room full of busloads of
tourists, a scene reminiscent of my Pennsylvania past. The
turkeys were nowhere to be found, beyond the menu and the
gift shop magnets.

After endless summers in Pennsylvania, I was excited to
go, at age nine, to Girl Scout camp instead. However, I was
considerably younger than my tentmates, who by then had
already learned a thing or two in junior high school about sexuality and their bodies. I was precocious in a somewhat different way; a tomboy, I had been caught staring at another
girl and, as a result, was an easy victim for the camp bullies.
They teased me mercilessly and tortured me in all the ways
girls find to humiliate each other.

I called my grandmother in tears.

"You must be exaggerating," she said. "Everyone is nice
underneath. I'm sure they all want to be your friends."
Insisting, she added, "Find the positive. Tell me one good
thing that has happened since you started camp."

I leaned into the phone and spoke quietly, so the line of
girls behind me wouldn't hear: "Well, Grandma, when the
girls made me sit under the tent, I found a wallet full of
money buried in the dirt."

"Oh." There was a pause. "In that case, let me put your
grandfather on the phone."

This was a new experience. I had never spoken to my
grandfather on the phone before, but it was clear that my
grandmother thought he was the one I should talk to. The
first thing he said was "You have to stop crying or I'll come
up there myself." Knowing that he might follow through on
this threat, and that he would do anything to defend me, for
the safety of all involved I took some deep breaths and
explained the situation. He came up with a plan: I was to use

the money to obtain personal security. I immediately hired two older campers for twenty dollars a week apiece, they beat up the kids who had been beating me up, and my summer significantly improved.

I came home relieved and fifteen pounds thinner, the result of lots of physical activity and, despite my expectations, no Girl Scout cookies. As volunteers on a kibbutz discover, everything good is for export.

As the next summer approached, I made it a point to look very busy. I hoped to be left alone, but my family had other plans. A gracious invitation from my father's family sent me (age twelve) and my brother (age nine) on an odyssey across the South. My parents gave us a total of nine hundred dollars in cash, and put us on a plane to my father's sister, who lived in Amarillo, Texas. The magic of this trip may best be captured through the description "*National Lampoon's Vacation* meets *Deliverance*."

We started off in Dallas, where we spent three days in the sun without a single drop of suntan lotion. Rather than seek out medical attention, our relatives splurged on a hotel room with air conditioning, probably out of fear that one of us would die. At the time, my brother had a short crew cut, and I am sure that his scalp, like my shoulders, is still scarred from a sun poisoning that resembled a makeover from *Leatherface*. Fortunately he retains a full head of hair.

As one of my cousins raided the minibar, I sat transfixed in front of the television watching *Jaws*, feeling the skin on my shoulders blister and crisp like a roasted chicken. As I prayed for a shark to eat me alive and put me out of my misery, desperation won. I snuck out to the van that pulled my aunt and uncle's RV and pinched one of my uncle's Schlitzes, still cool from its place in the cooler under the soft drinks. Self-medication made more sense than suicide, especially since I was absolutely sure that if I died I would be cremated so that my family wouldn't have to pay for transporting my broken body. Being half-burnt already, I had no interest in more heat. Three beers later, I was informed by the other hotel occupants that I was much better company.

The next morning, after we had taken excruciating showers, my aunt decided to give us a home remedy consisting of diluted milk of magnesia. We looked like the walking dead. Our ghoulish visage and lumbering movements caused anyone who saw us to take a deep breath and mumble something significant about one Jesus H. Christ. We were camera-ready for a voodoo ritual when we entered the Denny's in Vicksburg, Mississippi, covered in a thick crust of milk of magnesia. As the discussion at the kids' table turned to the graphic content in the new movie, *Children of the Corn*, my poor brother slipped under the table into a pallid dehydrated pile. I continued eating ketchup and syrup, waiting for the pancakes, which our cousin stole as soon as they arrived.

In Oklahoma, we were given sticks and strings and encouraged to catch our own supper. I caught a few sunnies, more bone than fish. My brother used the opportunity to better position himself politically with our family by trying chewing tobacco. My own attempts at acclimation largely consisted of acquiring a bad southern accent, but his were more successful. Skoal Bandits had never before been marked as a point of cultural prestige. While these little cancer packets were not part of our Yankee vocabulary, my brother did his best to fit in. To me, they tasted like salty and strangely compelling toothpaste mixed with dirt, and I quickly gave up.

One of our final stops was the New Orleans World Fair; there, I got lost and separated from the group. I decided to explore on my own before returning to where we had decided to meet at the end of the day. This seemed like a good idea, at first, but as the afternoon got hotter I found myself on a street full of liquor stores, with men loitering outside and glancing at me strangely. Looking up, I saw a pair of women's legs, made of papier mâché, dangling from the awning of a strip club, the most welcoming place I could find. The waitresses mistook me for a little boy and took pity on me, allowing me in before they opened, and giving me a drink of punch. We returned to New York from our southern odyssey wearing cowboy outfits. This was the lowest I had sunk in my twelve years. My aunt forced me and my brother into tight Lee jeans and cowboy hats—at least his outfit didn't include a frilled shirt. The stewardesses designated to oversee unescorted minors snickered as we languished on the four-hour flight.

Our parents met us at the airport. They were newly bright-eyed and bushy-tailed. In their exuberance at our absence, they had bought a new car: a 1984 Buick land whale, chosen for its unique shade of camouflage brown and a back seat big enough to keep me and my brother from fighting. The new-car smell, combined with a lack of beer cans clinking under my seat, felt like being in a limousine.

A few years later, I was relieved at the prospect of a vacation that would not involve family. I signed up for a high school trip billed as a multidisciplinary European adventure. The trip's original chaperone had been maimed in a terrible motorcycle accident, the week before we left, so an alternate was desperately sought. At the last moment, the mother of a brooding boy from my church graciously volunteered. An ex-pat German hausfrau, she came on this trip armed with five thousand dollars, in small bills, and a superhero-tight pair of lederhosen that left nothing to the imagination. This was the first trip in which I was left to my own devices to pack, and I equipped myself with three suitcases and a metric ton of mix tapes.

The trip began in Ludwigshafen, Germany. One of our first stops was in Munich, at the Hofbrauhaus. Upon reflection, I am not sure why a brewery that was a former Nazi hangout was on the itinerary for a group of American high school students. The beer flowed freely as inebriated tourists in various states of undress danced on the tables; one of them even caught a bra on his head, a bra designed for the most buxom of the Valkyries.

We were all encouraged to taste the beer. Some of us used straws taken from the hotel, to maximize our German beer hall experience. Our chaperone drank more than the rest of us put together. Happy to be back in her element, she led a nearby group from Oklahoma in songs reminiscent of better days of German yore. This was German beer, not the watered-down Budweiser you could get by sneaking into clubs with fake ID. We had never had real beer before. Our high school experimentations with drinking had involved either bottles of Gallo stolen from the basements of our homes or vain attempts to buy beer; to have it on tap was a dream come true, and we were hammered.

After a long night in the beer hall, we returned to our rooms. Our chaperone somehow ended up in mine. She was still singing when she fell asleep, face down in her lederhosen. Somewhere in the middle of the night, my roommate and I woke up. The chaperone had not moved, and we were absolutely sure that she was dead. We turned on the light, and still there was no motion. We started to sober up when we realized our predicament. Here we were, two high school kids in a hotel room in a foreign country, with a chaperone lying spreadeagle on the bed, dead of alcohol poisoning. No dabbler badge from the Girl Scouts could have prepared us for that moment, and nothing we had learned in German class equipped us with a suitable vocabulary. We could not even work the phones.

Convinced that she had experienced a rock-star-style demise, and scared at the premise of being involved in an international incident, we took matters into our own hands. We silently feared a college rejection based on felonious extracurricular activity. We had simply worked too hard to have our futures compromised by a dead woman stuffed into leather hot pants, however lovely she was in life.

My roommate calmly opened her compact and placed the mirror by the chaperone's nose. It took about a minute, but the mirror finally steamed up. The combination of relief (she was alive) and terror (she still was not moving), along with all the alcohol we had imbibed, required immediate use of the facilities. My roommate went first. When it was my turn, I stepped into the airline-sized bathroom and locked the door. Fumbling blindly for the light switch, I swiveled the wrong way and proceeded to pirouette and crack my head on the toilet bowl. I would remain on the bathroom floor, unconscious and oozing blood, until the morning, only to be woken up by a very hung-over chaperone—who I am sure was as worried about me as my roommate and I had been about her. At least I was not wearing leather pants.

My head was now slightly concave, dented to the point that I could never get a crew cut, out of fear of looking like bruised fruit. In college, I stood by quietly as my friends enjoyed their meaningful Sinead O'Connor phase, experimenting with baldness. I could not share their breezy and well-trimmed new hair style. I settled for an eggplant purple faux-hawk instead.

Looking back, it is strange to realize that on this high school trip to Germany, not a word about the Holocaust was spoken. There was an optional excursion to Dachau, but I chose not to go, and the kids who went came back shell-shocked and silent. Nothing was said to the group as a whole. Beginning our trip at the Hofbrauhaus, which had been a Nazi stronghold during the war, I saw the people singing and drinking beer all around me and had an intimation of a history of evil. Even from what little I knew, the hairs stood up on the back of my neck as I imagined the scene in that very room just fifty years before. But whenever I tried to ask questions, our chaperone and trip leaders would talk about something else. I knew there was more to the country's history than beer, but talking about it was taboo.

The silence was all the more uncomfortable for me because my father's family is German. My great-grandparents came from Germany to America after the First World War; I remember my great-grandmother's iron cross wedding ring, with the inscription *In times of trouble, I gave my Fatherland gold for iron*. She never learned English. There are family rumors that my great-grandfather, her husband, had Nazi leanings. Like many immigrants from Germany to America—including the Jewish Germans of that time—my great-grandparents kept their pride and patriotism, and their belief in German culture. By the time I was growing up, they and their daughter, my grandmother, were dead, and my father's two sisters lived far away. Unlike Germans who lived in Germany during the Holocaust, and the generations after, members of my American German family expressed no self-scrutiny, no reflection or remorse, about that period to me. The only connection is through some German books in my parents' basement, along with my father's collection of German stamps.

I did not truly learn about the Holocaust until after my high school trip, when a friend who was already in college gave me a copy of Viktor Frankl's book of suffering and survival, *Man's Search for Meaning*. A decade later, I would discover the personal impact of the Holocaust when I rented an apartment in Jerusalem from the daughter of a prominent Jewish communal leader who had died in Dachau. The way the Holocaust had shaped her life spoke volumes. I remembered that missed trip to Dachau as a teenager, and I knew that one day I would have to return to Germany. As a Jew, confronting the Holocaust would no longer be an optional side trip. And so it was that, five years after I met that survivor in Jerusalem, I took the opportunity to travel to Bendorf, in the Rhineland, for an international, interfaith conference. Instead of the Hofbrauhaus, the conference would be based at Hedwig-Dransfeld Haus, a center for dialogue and study. I was there as a rabbinical student, and the only American there.

My seminary, the Academy for Jewish Religion (AJR), was the sole rabbinical school in the United States to send students to this conference. As a school, AJR was very focused on Jewish pluralism and intrafaith dialogue; rabbinic and cantorial students came from across the denominational spectrum. I studied beside Jews who were Conservative and Orthodox, Reconstructionist, Reform, and Renewal, Jews who were postdenominational, and Jews who had lived within many different denominations. Our teachers also came from varied backgrounds.

I applied to the AJR rabbinical school upon returning from Pardes, the yeshiva where I studied in Jerusalem. At the time, I was living a traditional Jewish life, but, as a woman and a lesbian, I would not have been accepted into the more traditional seminaries. Moreover, I truly believed in the academy's mission. I wanted to learn from everyone. The school's motto, "The Torah has Many Faces," reflected the belief that everyone had something to contribute to the conversation. There was a deep commitment to dialogue of all sorts—hence the opportunity to go to Germany for the interfaith conference.

When I reached Dusseldorf, I had to wait in the airport for hours for the arrival of a group of English rabbinical students, with whom I would be sharing a bus. In the time it took for them to arrive, I rediscovered that German airports have terrible seating but fantastic pork, cheese, chocolate, and beer. I avoided the pork but was otherwise somewhat dizzy by the time the group arrived. They all knew each other, and had no interest in getting to know an American. Even at a conference celebrating religious and cultural differences, coming from the United States still put me beyond the pale. I experienced this throughout the conference, and particularly at the Jewish group's services. When I walked in for the evening prayers, I was met at the door by a burly, red-headed woman from the Ukraine, who informed me in a voice straight out of *Rocky IV* that I was not to assume any leadership, and that the prayers would be strictly run according to European tradition. It was the European equivalent of an Amish shunning.

Excommunicated by my own people, I went to the opening plenary feeling a little like Spinoza. The room was filled with people speaking many languages and wearing many forms of religious garb. Conversations and armpits were heated, and everyone in the room needed to shave; it was like being in the bar in *Star Wars*. This year's opening exercise involved being asked to choose the animal that best represented our religion. One Palestinian participant decided to compare his people to wolves, which, in his words, "would chew off their own legs for freedom"; the room got significantly hotter. This was not the warm interreligious dialogue I had imagined in my naiveté, and I found myself wondering why I had crossed the ocean for the same arguments I could find in New York. As my claustrophobia reached a fever pitch, I debated leaving the next morning. I asked God for a sign. Across the room, I noticed some people climbing into the overfilled session through a ground-floor window. Something about one of them caught my eye, as she tumbled into the room. I smiled, thinking of my grandmother's saying: "God closes a door, and throws you out the window." For the first time in years, the window felt wide open.

Planting Seeds: The Tree of Life

The next morning, I met Lisa. We were at the first group service, which all the participants were required to attend. It was Catholic, involving incense and other things that set off my asthma. The room filled with smoke, reminding me of an Egyptian plague.

And then, I heard it: the voice of God. As a Christian, I had always appreciated men's stained-glass voices, the richness of tone and timbre, how people could use their voices to elevate the spoken word. The Jewish circles I had moved in were much more down to earth. And, although I had been around many female clergy, I had never heard that voice from a woman. I couldn't even look at her—I froze and just listened. I was facing forward, and everything went black. I listened to the cadence of her speech, and I recognized the accent right away: Canadian. I turned around, and there she was, the woman who had come in through the window the night before. Now she was trying to describe her thesis to the woman sitting between us, who in turn was feigning interest. To be fair, she had asked. But to ask a graduate student about her thesis is like asking a hypochondriac how they're feeling: it won't be a short answer. Fortunately, this bought me some time. "There's a fascinating apocryphal Christian text which related to the biblical passage," she was saying. "How better could Mary's virginity be proven than through a public exoneration of adultery?"

It was the beginning of a beautiful relationship. Even today, we marvel that two rabbis-to-be met on German soil, that a country that would have killed us for being gay and being Jews became the fertile ground for our romance. Had my father's parents not left Germany, and had Lisa's grandparents and great-grandparents not left Eastern Europe, my relatives might have killed hers. And yet there we were, in the days that followed the Catholic service, taking walks through the woods in the Rhineland spring, seeing the green leaves begin to unfurl on the trees, and starting something new.

After the week of the conference was complete, Lisa returned to her studies in Oxford, and I resumed my life in

New York. We then had three months of trans-Atlantic correspondence, which included Lisa sending me novels and packets of tea, and me sending her my prized set of Greek-English Josephus translations, twelve small volumes in twelve small packages finding their way across the ocean. We emailed each other about everything from the Gospel of Mark to the stories of our lives. I mentioned that I had frequent flyer miles, and she invited me to come.

I went to visit Lisa in Oxford. The promise of *The Twig* had been fulfilled, and she was there as her high school's twentieth Rhodes Scholar. The trip was our equivalent of a U-Haul date. I knew I had found the person with whom I would spend the rest of my life when we went grocery shopping, and, totally unselfconsciously, she paused at the milk section and said, "We've been buying 1 percent for years." It felt like we had been together forever.

Our first day together in Oxford, Lisa took me punting on the River Thames. As she tried valiantly not to run over any ducklings, I stayed very still trying not to tip the boat or hit my head on any bridges. My anglophilia was only slightly tempered by my various concussions on the trip, knocking my head on the staircase leading to the top of the Sheldonian Theatre, on college doorways, and on the low-hanging beams of the inn where we stayed in Hay-on-Wye. The signs on the medieval buildings read "Mind your head," a phenomenological reminder that I never processed quite quickly enough. Lisa, meanwhile, loved living in England, if only because, for the first time in her life, she didn't feel short, since everything was built for someone her size. When I eventually met Lisa's grandmother, a woman less than five feet tall, she looked me up and down and said, "Well, at least you can reach things." She promptly asked me to get some dishes down from her top cabinet, and that was my welcome to the family.

The next spring, Lisa and I returned to the conference in Germany together. We taught a study session on Jonah and a little-known biblical figure named Serach bat Asher. In Midrash, Serach is transformed from a minor character to a musician, historian, and sage, blessed with longevity and given a crucial role in the story of the Israelites' redemption. We also introduced our Jewish, Christian, and Muslim colleagues to the concept of bibliodrama: acting out interpretations of the Torah. To our fascination, we discovered that the Muslims would do anything except play the part of God, while the Jews and Christians fought over the privilege. The German Christian contingent commandeered the conference center's tablecloths to dress up as Egyptians and enact Moses' early years, and Lisa and I stood back to watch the drama unfold. It was the first of many times we would teach together and bring people together whose paths would not have otherwise crossed. The participants' differences were plain to see, even when draped in linens. You could tell the Germans from the Egyptians from the Brits, the Christians from the Muslims from the Jews. To all of them, the two of us probably looked alike: two Jewish women with short brown hair and glasses. Only we knew how far we had come to be together.

Tu B'Shevat, the Jewish New Year of Trees, originated as the time on the calendar from which the age of trees was calculated for purposes of tithing. In these post-tithing times, this date has become the Jewish celebration of trees and the natural world. The birth of a tree is less violent and bloody than the birth of a human being, but no less dramatic. It takes years before you see flowers or fruit; all the same, you know something new has begun. Growth is not assured, but when a tree does flourish, it affects generations.

The moment that Lisa and I met in Bendorf, the seeds were planted for that night when we would sit across the kitchen table from each other and dust off our yearbooks, *The*

Lance and *The Twig*. The seeds were also planted for other late nights, awake not with our books but with our children. There is a Talmudic story of an old man named Honi. An emperor passed by him one day when he was planting a tree. "Why do you plant this tree," the emperor asked, "when you will probably not live to see its fruit?" "My ancestors planted trees for me," Honi replied, "so I plant for those who will come after." We continue to expect the unexpected.

4

The New Year for Animals

Because No One Is Allergic to Butterflies

On the first of Elul is the New Year for the Tithe of Cattle (Rabbi Eleazar and Rabbi Shimon say: The first of Tishrei).   —Mishnah Rosh Hashanah 1:1

Who gives us more knowledge than the beasts of the earth, makes us wiser than the birds of the sky?
    —Job 35:11

Risky Raccoons and Nut-Free Cats

Dear Kindergarten Parents,

Today while the students were at the park, the teachers saw a raccoon walking around the play area. While the raccoon did not show any evident signs of disease, they believed that it was prudent to keep our students away from it. As soon as the raccoon was spotted, the teachers had the students line up and everyone left the park quickly and safely. Many of the children saw the raccoon and may talk about it tonight. We did talk to the children about how they were all safe and you should know that none of the children touched the raccoon. If you have any further questions or concerns about what happened, please do not hesitate to contact us.

Thank you,
Your Child's Jewish Day School

No book, magazine, or childrearing guide could prepare a parent for this email. There is no *What to Expect When Your Child Encounters a Raccoon in the Park*. In the YouTube of my mind, I imagined this raccoon sashaying through Central Park, not dissimilar from a kindergarten child. Both are playful scavengers who are too often nocturnal, with prehensile thumbs, prone to loitering near the sandbox. I envisioned the encounter between the species: the mutual curiosity, the heightened interest, the wondering whether the other either has—or is—food. The battle over turf. The little noses sniffing in the air. The inevitable parting of ways. I wondered whether the raccoon went home to tell its family about the excitement as well.

My first reaction was relief that everything was fine, and the realization that I would in fact kill a small animal with my bare hands if it threatened my child. For a brief moment, I felt a spark of connection to my grandfather, sitting with a BB gun pointed out of his bedroom window and monitoring the street below. I also felt a sense of gratitude that the school clearly was on top of the situation. Local newspapers had reported a recent spike in incidents involving rabid animals in Central Park. If the school took such precautions with a raccoon, I could only begin to imagine the other ways they protected my child.

Then I grew excited. "Many of the children saw the raccoon and may talk about it tonight." Maybe tonight would be the night our daughter would tell us something when we asked her about her day at school. If nothing else, I now had what the teachers called a "prompt," a topic to start with in my attempts to elicit information.

Next, I started to wonder how many ways this encounter could have ended. If there had been a class from a culinary institute or a cultural academy, instead of a kindergarten class, would the raccoon have ended up as dinner, in honor of some heritage day? I imagined the free-range raccoon on a platter, with essence of a locally sourced vegetable sauce on the side. What would the reaction have been from my own elementary school teachers and class?

Where I grew up, on Long Island, animals were less worthy of note. My primary school was not quite 4H, but there was a fair amount of contact with the animal world. There were class mealworms and class mice, quail that were raised by one student's family and warranted a field trip to their house. Class animals went home with children on a rotating basis.

My family was notorious for killing them. Whenever it was our turn, something died. Two adult mice, a number of baby mice, and one gerbil met their end within our walls. As far as we know, they died of heat exhaustion due to the Amish absence of air conditioning in our suburban home. Looking back, the fact that they were always kept on my bedroom dresser, in a large patch of sunlight with a mirror behind their cage, probably didn't help. It was like being under a magnifying glass all day in the sun. My mother tried icing them down, which only killed them faster and left us with rodents that were not only dead but also cold and wet. One mouse came to us pregnant, and within a few hours had a litter of new babies. In the morning, we discovered that she had eaten some in the night; by afternoon, the rest had succumbed to the heat. For two weeks after, visions of mouse ghosts danced through my head, and I was afraid to reenter my room. We were taken off the lists of animal hosts and referred to in hushed tones as "the family where things go to die." We had killed Skippy, Mrs. Skippy, and their brood. The teachers did not welcome the burden of being pet-loss counselors on top of their already full workload.

At my daughter's school, allergies and indemnity prevent living things other than children to enter the classroom. There are no class pets. Instead, the nursery children were sent home with a stuffed dog named Pretzel and a notebook intended to record the adventures of this class "pet" with each family. The notebook also provided an opportunity for parents to compare their children's fledgling handwriting and catch voyeuristic glimpses into each other's apartments and lives.

I was more afraid of Pretzel than I was of Skippy and family. Bringing him into our own home, with three real animals (two cats and one dog), seemed like tempting fate. I wondered how he might get defiled or destroyed. Worse, I was afraid he would become the Typhoid Mary of allergies, bringing back real fur alongside his hypoallergenic stuffing. I went over him with a HEPA filter before returning him, in absolute fear that whoever would have him next would blame us. Lisa had similar nightmares, but, as family lunch-maker, she had them in the form of imagining accidentally packing something containing nuts in our daughter Ariella's lunch.

The cats are furry, but thankfully nut-free. We took care of that when we got them. One, Mika, is also blind, and the other, Moka, is missing teeth, and neither have their claws. Between the two cats, there is less than one set of working parts. We didn't know that Mika was blind until we moved the furniture and he started walking into walls. We took him to the vet, who, trying to break the news gently, said, "He's not visual right now." "What does that mean?" we asked. It turns out what it means is that his eyes are not attached to his brain; in other words, there is no hope of him becoming visual before the messianic age. All the same, Mika rules the roost, regularly beating up the dog, who is four times his size. The three animals have a clearly defined social hierarchy, which is why we get apprehensive about disturbing the peace whenever we are asked to bring even a stuffed one home.

The next animal to come to us was Dov Bear. Whereas Pretzel had arrived on a weekday, Dov Bear—complete with notebook—came on Shabbat. This upped the ante considerably, especially since he was sent to our home first. The two rabbis had to set the bar high, and neither of us remembered any rabbinical school classes on how to treat stuffed animals on Shabbat. So we welcomed Dov Bear like any other guest. We lit candles, sipped grape juice, and ate challah. We were careful to keep him far from any pets or nuts, and a good time was had by all.

Stuffed animals were one way schools avoided the animal allergy quandary. Another way involved insects. Our first introduction to the "bugs as a class pet" idea took the form of weekly photographs sent to us on the first Friday of Ariella's summer camp at the local Y. After a few conventional shots of kids playing, came a large yellow close-up of boxes of larvae, boxes that read in large red letters "Attention: Live Insects—Handle with Care—Do Not Freeze." There was no caption. A number of parents were confused, and checked and rechecked backpacks to make sure this was not a take-home assignment. The kids in the class could barely walk, never mind explain the concept of metamorphosis. They were at the stage where they simply couldn't come home and tell us what was going on, as opposed to the precocious preteenage phase, which would strike two years later, when they could tell us but made a conscious decision not to. The next week, we learned from the counselors that the group was raising ladybugs, which would be liberated in a rooftop ceremony. That week's set of photographs included children joyfully releasing the ladybugs into the trees. The bugs were flying upward, like doves being liberated at a peace festival or a wedding. Within a few moments, thanks to a lack of fine motor skills on the part of the children and the bugs, combined with an unfortunate wind, there was inevitable blowback, squishing, and likely ingestion. Ariella came home blissfully unaware of the bits of ladybugs in her hair, ladybugs that hadn't quite made it to freedom. The horror of that moment was to remain only with the grown-ups. The memory Ariella carries is of the ladybug that came back and landed on her knee to visit her before saying a sweet goodbye.

After ladybugs, we graduated to butterflies. The nursery class raised monarchs and released them in the park. We had the opportunity to do the same the next year during Ariella's pre-kindergarten year, when Lisa's parents surprised us with caterpillars in the mail. Feeling that our house was already full enough, we shared them with the class, grateful that the teacher was willing to accept these entomological refugees. The caterpillar kit guaranteed that, of the five Painted Lady caterpillars which arrived, at least three would become "happy adult butterflies." To this day, I am not sure how one measures butterfly happiness; we would count it as success if three of the five remained alive. After that, they would be responsible for their own emotional well-being. Every morning, Ariella pressed her nose against the plastic jar, checking to see how many survived.

In truth, we could not control the butterflies' survival, much less their happiness, and we could not keep our children from crossing paths with wayward raccoons. As the parent of an allergy-free child, I can only imagine what it is like to send someone you love into a world riddled with threats. And I wonder how much of the tone of post-9/11 New York is shaped by trying to protect our children from the things we *can* control, in the face of so much that we cannot.

In some ways, our children are remarkably sophisticated. If you ask nursery students at Ariella's school what their favorite tree is, they are likely to say "gingko biloba"; if you ask them their favorite activity, "yoga" may well be the response. These children eat sushi and hail taxis with aplomb. Looking through a Wonder Woman comic book,

Ariella saw a storyline featuring Nazis with their arms extended in salute. "Are they trying to hail a cab?" she asked. One of Ariella's friends was with his older stepsister, who asked him to turn his back while she changed; "Don't worry," said the boy, fresh from a summer at a camp where the children change into their bathing suits in the halls. "I see vaginas all the time."

In other ways, these children are more protected than any generation before. Every parent has some quirk, whether it is the number of years the child is kept in a car seat or the length of time the child is kept from chewing gum. "Is this dog friendly?" we tell our children to ask, and yet we all know that friendly dogs can still bite.

The Book of Jonah, which is read on the afternoon of Yom Kippur, also uses animals to teach some lessons on what we can and cannot control. God gives Jonah a mission, to tell the people of Nineveh to repent. Jonah does not like the Ninevites and does not want the job; thinking he can run from God, he takes a ship in the opposite direction from where he has been sent. In response, God sends a big fish to swallow the reluctant prophet. A rabbinic Midrash imagines Jonah being taken on an underwater tour around the world. He sees hell below and the Temple above, the origins of the earth and of the sea, and the foundation stone of the world. The message of Jonah's trip is similar to God's response to Job, reminding him of his own smallness in the face of the majesty and mystery of creation. In both cases, it seems God is telling us how little we ultimately understand, and how little is in our control. If you give God the car keys, you have to let God drive.

At the end of the Book of Jonah, the prophet succeeds in his mission to turn the Ninevites to repentance, but his happiness is, unlike the promise of butterfly kit, far from guaranteed. He is angry that he had to make the journey, angry that the Ninevites repented, and angry that the giant gourd that God gave him for shade has shriveled up and died. God uses this as a teaching moment: "Then the Eternal said: 'You cared about the plant, which you did not work for and which you did not grow, which appeared overnight and perished overnight. And should not I care about Nineveh, that great city, in which there are more than a hundred and twenty thousand persons who do not yet know their right hand from their left, and many beasts as well?" (Jonah 4:10–11). There is so much that is not in human control, God says, and yet that is precisely why we should care. Living in a potentially rabid world, we try to keep our children from touching what they shouldn't touch, and we give them the sense that they are safe. But, as a parent and as a rabbi, I also want to teach them what we can do to make the world a better place.

I come from a family in which nature was not seen as a friend. Our motto was "He who bites first, lasts." The memories of Skippy and family make me narcoleptic whenever Ariella goes to a nature center or petting zoo. Bugs make me squirm, and the arrival of a stuffed animal and a notebook in her backpack is enough to throw me for a loop. And yet, if one of those experiences can help to make her a mensch, I will do whatever it takes.

Scabby the Rat

Our teacher Rabbi Judah haNasi was sitting and studying the Torah in front of the Babylonian Synagogue in Sepphoris, when a calf passed before him on its way to the slaughter and began to cry out, "Save me!" He said to it, "What can I do for you? For this you were made." As a punishment for his heartlessness, our teacher suffered toothaches for thirteen years . . . After this period a creeping thing ran past his daughter. She was about to kill it, when he said to her, "My daughter, let it be, for it is written, 'And God's tender mercies are over all of God's works'" (Psalm 145:9).

—Genesis Rabbah 33:3

The encounter with the raccoon resulted in an emergency email. Scabby the Rat, however, was outside the school for weeks and received no mention. Scabby, a union rat, was a fifteen-foot-tall balloon in front of a construction site across the road from Ariella's school. It was there to protest the management's employment of nonunion labor. Granted, it posed no actual threat to the children, but it was fairly horrifying to look at. With its sharp teeth, bloodshot eyes, outstretched claws, and infected teats, it was designed to generate revulsion. It soon became a favorite landmark for Ariella's walk to school. The hardened adult urban reaction may be to ignore the union rat and notice the stray raccoon, but the kids pay attention to everything. And so our routine expanded to include discussions of both politics and anatomy. Ariella noticed when the balloon was different—there were two models, alternating with no discernible pattern—and she asked countless questions: Why is he here? Do subway rats grow this big? Why is he alone? Why don't other rats want to come and play with him? Where does Scabby go at night? Does he have someone to cook dinner for him?

A curious kindergartener, Ariella was genuinely concerned about the health and well-being of the nonunion rat. She wanted to see more of these rats, so she would know that Scabby had friends. She thought that the inflation machine was a respirator and that Scabby needed a doctor. If there was a day he was not there, she worried about him and wanted to know where he had gone. I had been pulling her to the other side of the street, worried that she would be afraid of the rat and hoping it would just go away, but she was fascinated. Scabby was different and Scabby was big, but Scabby was worthy of care.

Beyond the outflow of compassion, seeing Scabby inspired some of Ariella's first conversations about social justice. Standing in front of the rat, she asked me what it was doing there. The union protester who was handing out pamphlets replied, "We're doing the right thing, sweetie." It took more for her to understand what a giant inflatable rat had to do with doing the right thing. We spoke about unions and workers' rights. "Just because you work for someone," I told her, "doesn't mean they own you." We spoke about free speech, a conversation that at first led Ariella to believe that not having free speech meant that you have to pay every time you talk. She loved the concepts of having the right to say what you want, and of speaking up when you see something wrong. She learned, like Rabbi Judah in the story with the calf, that it is not a sufficient answer to say, in the face of suffering: "What can I do? This is just the way things are."

One summer, when Ariella was two, she and Lisa saved a worm. They were rushing out of our apartment building on their way to camp, and Ariella spotted a worm inside the building. "Take care, worm!" she commanded. Lisa slid the worm onto an envelope, and moved it to the paved area outside the building. Ariella wouldn't budge. "Take care, worm!" she commanded again. So Lisa moved it up onto the grass. "Take care, worm!" Ariella insisted, unwilling to leave. It was not until Lisa had positioned the worm under a bush on the soil, in a prime section of worm real estate, that Ariella was willing to move on. As Lisa tells the story, she had been in a hurry to get out the door to camp, but Ariella taught her that there was something much more important at stake: there was a worm that needed help, and the job needed to be done right. Thanks to Ariella, they fixed a little bit of the world that morning.

The Baal Shem Tov, the founder of Chasidism, taught: "In what way is a human being superior to a worm? A worm serves the Creator with all of his intelligence and ability; and man, too, is compared to a worm. . . . If God had not given you a human intellect, you would only be able to serve God like a worm. In this sense, you are both equal in the eyes of Heaven. A person should consider himself, the worm, and all creatures as friends in the universe, for we are all created beings whose abilities are God-given" (*Tzava'at HaRivash* 12). Maybe it is because they are closer to the ground, or maybe it is something more profound, but children have a tendency to see animals as fellow travelers. It is not inevitable that they want to care for them; for some children, the instinct to squash them is equally strong. But the potential to develop a sense of compassion and a sense of justice is something to be nurtured.

The Red Heifer and the White Dog

Rabban Gamaliel, Rabbi Elazar ben Azaria, Rabbi Joshua, and Rabbi Akiva were coming up to Jerusalem together, and when they reached Mount Scopus, they tore their garments. When they got to the Temple Mount and saw a jackal emerging from the Holy of Holies, they began to weep, but Rabbi Akiva laughed. "Why," they asked him, "are you laughing?" He replied, "Why are you weeping?" They said, "This holy place is now become the haunt of jackals. Should we not weep?" He said to them, "For that very reason, I am laughing . . . now that the prophecy of destruction has been fulfilled, it is quite certain that the prophecy of rebuilding also is to be fulfilled." They said to him, "Akiva, you have comforted us! Akiva, you have comforted us!"   —Babylonian Talmud, Makkot 24b

Just as the sighting of a jackal was a sign of desolation on the Temple Mount, so too do animals make many appearances in children's books about death. Whether *Goodbye Mousie* or *The Tenth Good Thing about Barney*, a book with animal characters gives parents and children ways to talk about mortality. Ariella is used to both her mothers going to officiate at funerals; once, she went so far as to insist, with the certitude only a five-year-old can have, "I am an expert on funerals." But, for other parents, for whom death is not a part of daily life, the topic can be harder to raise. A number of families cross the road in the school's neighborhood so as to walk in front of the Jewish Community Center instead of the local funeral home. It is easier to explain grown-ups running endlessly on treadmills than a hearse containing a coffin in which a person is finally still. All the same, the day comes when the dead goldfish has to be flushed down the toilet, or the dog's final trip to the vet must be explained. I have been asked to do a funeral for a cat; in that case, I used catnip for the spices at havdalah, the ceremony marking the end of Shabbat. And as a rabbi, I have spoken with children about how one of the Jewish images of heaven is *Gan Eden*, the Garden of Eden. If it is truly the Garden of Eden, our animals too must have a place there.

In Judaism, there is a fascinating intersection between one specific kind of animal and rituals around death. In the Torah, we learn about the red heifer. A young cow that is entirely red and unblemished, and which has never worn a yoke, is killed and burned to ashes. Those ashes are then used in a ceremony to purify those who have come into contact with death. There are many puzzling aspects to this ritual: Why a red heifer? And how does the death of one creature help purify a person from the death of another? If nothing else, we learn the lengths to which we are willing to go to mourn and then move forward. The *Tosefta*, an early rabbinic compilation, shows keen psychological insight when it notes: "not to mourn is impossible, but if you mourn too much you are mourning for something else." Grief is expressed, but mourning is limited by the passage of time and the other requirements of religious life. Shiva, the seven days of mourning traditionally observed at home following a funeral, is interrupted by Shabbat, and ended by a holiday. And, instead of the calendar being taken over by all the tragedies our people have accumulated over the millennia of our history, our remembrances are concentrated on one fast day, Tisha b'Av. Even during the existential depths of Yom Kippur, we are reminded to choose life. One of the classic Jewish teachings is that, if a funeral procession and a wedding procession meet in the road, the funeral gives way for the wedding. It is astonishing how many times that teaching is relevant, as many people find overlaps between moments of loss and moments of celebration.

Animals help us to acknowledge death, and also to make room for life. Some of the liveliest moments in our home have come thanks to our animals. One summer morning, Lisa was away at a clergy retreat. Since her specialty when it comes to cooking is breakfast, I was trying to make up for her absence by making pancakes for Ariella. I took out all the supplies, along with some toppings for a special treat, whipped cream and Nutella. It was early in the morning, not historically my best time of day, and I was having trouble reading the side of the pancake box. When I leaned in to read the fine print, I accidentally inhaled some of the powder. This led to the longest sneeze of my life, the kind where time stops and your brain explodes.

The powder went all over me. Temporarily blinded, I heard a hissing sound in the background, followed by the dog, Chewy, whimpering, Ariella giggling, and more hissing. Then I heard the pitter-patter of not-so-little feet, six at least, coming closer. I tried to blow the powder off my glasses so I could see. Out of the corner of my eye, I glimpsed the dog running, followed by the child. Both seemed to blend in more than usual with the off-white wall.

When they came around the turn for their second lap, I got a closer look. Chewy was covered with something white and Ariella was completely nude, except for smears of the same substance that was covering the dog. It was then that I realized there was whipped cream everywhere: on the dog, on the child, on the walls. The cats cowered under a chair, like people taking refuge from a blizzard, as Ariella and Chewy circled around them in gusty swirls of white. I ran through the whipped-cream storm to put a towel on the couch and turn on the television: this took care of the child. Now I had to catch the dog. I grabbed another towel, got him by his collar, and brought him to the door of the apartment, hoping to wipe him down in the hall. Resplendent in his greased-up glory, he instead slipped out of his collar and bolted out the door. In that moment, Ariella decided to make a run for it as well.

We live on the fourth floor of our building, and the stairs are right beside our door. Ariella went up, and the dog went down; I quickly decided to chase her first. Racing up the stairs, I grabbed her under one arm, and ran down the stairs to grab him. Climbing back up to our floor, a thirty-pound child under one arm and a thirty- pound dog under the other, I finally made it back to the door. The only thing louder than their indignant kvetching was the wheezing of my newly powdered, overexerted lungs.

Our neighbor chose exactly that moment to come out of her apartment. Mrs. McTavish was in her nineties and had lived in the building since she was a young bride during the Second World War. We always made an effort to hold doors open for her and help her on the stairs, only to be regaled with stories of the good old days, before Jews were allowed into the building. We didn't know whether she had noticed the mezuzah on our door—or, for that matter, that we were both women. In any case, all her worst stereotypes about "those people" ruining the neighborhood were confirmed by the sight of me, clad only in a tee-shirt and shorts, covered in whipped cream and pancake powder, and holding a squirming naked child and a very slippery dog.

I managed to get everyone inside and locked the door. Ariella went back down on the couch. I brought Chewy into the bathroom, turned on the water in the tub, and put him inside it to wash him. He looked up at me with his big brown eyes, and proceeded to make the biggest bowel movement of his life. This was the crap that broke the camel's back, leaving me up the proverbial creek without a paddle. I did, however, have a *New Yorker* magazine. Thinking quickly, I removed the address label, scooped the poop, and threw it all out the window. I spent the next three hours cleaning, channeling my inner Lady Macbeth. Once everything was calm, I sent Lisa a photo I had taken of Chewy covered with whipped cream. She stepped out of her meeting to send me an urgent text, "Is everything okay?" "Fine," I replied. And so it was.

The great Jewish theologian, Rabbi Abraham Joshua Heschel, speaks about experiencing the world through "radical amazement" and approaching it with a sense of awe and wonder. We live in a world that is both tragic and funny, in which terror and beauty often are very close. When we see the jackal on the Temple Mount, it is all too easy to see the destruction and not to see the hope. Heschel teaches us to see both. Watching Ariella with animals has taught me to see both. I have seen children jumping after ladybugs in the same way they would play with a dog; I have seen Ariella's absolute awe at a butterfly landing on her hand, or a caterpillar climbing her dress, on the way to *Tashlikh* services at the lake on Rosh Hashanah. For all that there is to be afraid of—for all that we adults are afraid of—we make way for our children's joy.

5

Sukkot

Wild Turkey

Mark, on the fifteenth day of the seventh month, when you have gathered in the yield of your land, you shall observe the festival of the Eternal seven days: a complete rest on the first day, and a complete rest on the eighth day. On the first day you shall take the product of citron trees, branches of palm trees, boughs of leafy trees, and willows of the brook, and you shall rejoice before the Eternal your God seven days. You shall observe it as a festival of the Eternal for seven days in the year; you shall observe it in the seventh month as a law for all time, throughout the ages. You shall live in booths seven days; all citizens in Israel shall live in booths, in order that future generations may know that I made the Israelite people live in booths when I brought them out of the land of Egypt, I the Eternal your God.　　　　　　—Leviticus 23:39–43

The Search for *Skhakh*:
To Boldly Go Where No Man Has Gone Before

The morning after my first Yom Kippur in Jerusalem, I woke up transformed, ready to begin my life anew. After a day full of services and conversations that went late into the night, I was bleary-eyed but inspired. I reached over to turn on my tape player and begin my morning ritual.

The familiar sounds of "O Mio Babbino Caro" filled the room as I enjoyed a Middle Eastern, Merchant Ivory moment. I jumped out of bed ready to greet the new day, singing the libretto as if the world was my shower. I was thousands of miles away from everything I knew. Anything felt possible, and I had a room with a view.

Over the music, I heard a faint rustling in the palm canopy outside my bedroom window. Perhaps it was the first warm rain of the season hitting the leaves, or the sounds of birds enjoying the pendulous date clusters hanging from the tree-top. Propelled by a heady combination of low blood sugar and an inflated sense of romantic grandeur, I twirled over to the windows. Flinging them wide, I half-expected to feast my eyes on my own private Duomo. The soprano Kiri Te Kanawa reached her crescendo, and I found myself eye-level with a hirsute Israeli man perched in the tree, hacking at the branches with a machete. I became acutely aware that I was wearing only a tank top and Superman Underoos.

"Skhakh, skhakh!" the man grumbled dismissively, shooing me away with his free hand as he continued to chop the palm fronds off the tree. In true Israeli fashion, he went about his business, ignoring me completely. It was perfectly normal to begin the day after Yom Kippur foraging for skhakh, the branches, leaves, and other foliage needed for the upcoming holiday of Sukkot. The holiday takes its name from the sukkah, a temporary dwelling built for the week-long holiday; skhakh provides a permeable roof for this provisional structure.

Religious requirements for foliage aside, this was not how I expected to begin my day. The stark reality remained: my palm tree, a thing of beauty and my only source of privacy, had just been given a mullet. I was in my underwear, and there was a strange man with a weapon outside my window who refused to leave. The thin butch veneer I had honed through college vanished in an instant, and I screamed at a volume that made my New York City heritage proud. Truly this was a scream that said "I am capable of anything and may be armed with Mace"—and with that I got his attention.

He started screaming almost as loudly as I. He dropped his machete, skittered down the tree, collected the palm fronds, and fled. I closed the window, ran into my bathroom, and assumed the fetal position. This was not the idyllic spiritual rebirth I had imagined. It was, however, my introduction to Sukkot in Jerusalem.

The man outside my window had been doing the right thing. In Judaism, the thing to do after Yom Kippur is not to prolong your spiritual reflection; rather, it is to get ready for the next holiday, Sukkot. The first mitzvah you are supposed to do after Yom Kippur is to begin to build your sukkah. As one early rabbinic teaching says, "From the Day of Atonement to the Feast of Booths all Israel are busy with the performance of religious duties. One is busy with his sukkah, one with his *lulav*" (Leviticus Rabbah 30:7).

Growing up, I knew the holiday only from its more Christian English appellation, the Feast of Tabernacles. As a child, I asked my mother what a Tabernacle was. "It's a choir," she replied, "in Utah." I decided that they must have been very special to merit such a transdenominational feast.

It was at Brandeis that I had my first encounter with Sukkot. I was drawn in by the fall foliage and the strings of fake fruit. Actually, I was drawn in by a cute Jewish girl who lived in my dorm and invited me to see the sukkah in the courtyard of the cafeteria. I was fascinated by the idea of *hiddur mitzvah*, taking something that is commanded and making it beautiful. Most of all, I was struck by the way people were taking part in building and decorating the sukkah, singing and laughing side by side with Jews from different backgrounds. This combination of religion and fun was a revelation to me, and it played a major role in my decision to explore Jewish life.

But now here I was in Jerusalem, hiding in the bathtub while a strange man harvested skhakh outside my window in celebration of the same holiday. Eventually I mustered the strength to venture forth. All pretenses of spirituality were dropped. It was time for shopping therapy. I hoped that the long walk to Ben Yehudah Street would calm me down. A touristy section of Jerusalem, it is a pedestrian mall full of small shops with conventional merchandise. I wanted to take refuge in the predictable postcards, IDF tee-shirts, wooden camels, and generic ritual items.

When I arrived later that morning, however, everything had changed. The usual products were pushed aside in favor of construction tools, plastic fruit, palm fronds, bamboo mats, and shiny decorations, all in preparation for Sukkot. The decorations were especially striking. Looking around, I saw I was not the only North American who was perplexed. The Sukkot decorations had more than a passing resemblance to the campiest Christmas trimmings.

Because of my experience with Sukkot at Brandeis, I had high expectations for my first celebration of this holiday in Jerusalem. It was in Massachusetts that I had learned to love nature, reading the transcendentalists and discovering Walden Pond; Sukkot was the perfect holiday for New England in autumn. I had not realized how different Jerusalem would be. Instead of fall foliage for skhakh, there were the palm fronds pillaged from outside my window; instead of multicolored dried corn and gourds, there were these kitschy Christmas decorations. As I continued walking down Ben Yehudah that day, I encountered other unexpected aspects of the holiday: salesmen summoning me into back alleys to buy the best etrog, for more money than my monthly rent, and men driving cars with skhakh strapped on top like a dead animal after a hunting trip. Without realizing it, my conception of Sukkot was entirely based in America: I felt myself a proud inheritor of a tradition in which Sukkot was the basis for Thanksgiving and everyone existed peacefully side by side. Sukkot in Jerusalem was a stark reminder of the very different world I had entered.

As my shock wore off, I was increasingly fascinated by the tinsel hanging from the model sukkahs, and by the pictures of revered rabbis covered with garlands. Going from store to store, I started to notice a theme. It was not only modern rabbis whose portraits were decorated this way; there were also row after row of pictures to be hung in the sukkah, tableaus of faces. The characters were all major biblical figures, but, from one stand to the next, they looked completely different. There was a Chasidic-looking Abraham, a Yemenite Abraham, a Modern Orthodox Abraham, a Kibbutznik Abraham. . . . The entire diversity of the Jewish people was portrayed. The only thing the images did not resemble were the depictions in the Bible that my family had given me as a child, in which the protagonists looked suspiciously Western European and blond.

When I asked a vendor on Ben Yehudah Street what these pictures were about, he did his best to explain them to me. "They are *ushpizin*," he said. "What's ushpizin?" He answered, "We invite in the dead." "Oh, so it's like Halloween." "No, the famous dead. From the Bible." This was my introduction to the concept of ushpizin, the forefathers and other significant figures from biblical history who are symbolically invited to come join the celebrants in the sukkah.

With all the culture clashes, I took great comfort—and great interest—in the idea of ushpizin. Ushpizin gave the whole holiday a new dimension and made it much more poignant. The Sukkot/Thanksgiving connection didn't quite make sense at Brandeis, but the connections I discovered on Ben Yehudah Street were much more profound.

As I learned more, I discovered that the seven traditional ushpizin—Abraham, Isaac, Jacob, Joseph, Moses, Aaron, and David—were chosen because they all left home and spent time wandering. For them, a temporary dwelling was especially appropriate. Like most biblical figures, they also were morally complicated but profoundly important, simultaneously heroic and flawed. They seemed as if they could be my relatives.

Most explanations of the four different species used on Sukkot—etrog, palm, myrtle, and willow—interpret them as representing four different kinds of Jews, or four different parts of the body. The idea is that we find strength through diversity, and that everyone and everything should come together in the service of God. But there is one other explanation, which uses wordplay to connect each of the four species to a different patriarch or matriarch from our people's past:

> *Hadar* symbolizes Abraham, whom the Holy One, blessed be God, honored him (*hiddero*) with good old age; as it says, "And Abraham was old, well stricken in age" (Gen. 24:1). . . . "Branches (*kappot*) of palm trees" symbolizes Isaac who had been tied (*kafut*) and bound upon the altar. "And boughs of thick trees" symbolizes Jacob; just as the myrtle is crowded with leaves so was Jacob crowded with children. "And willows of the brook" symbolizes Joseph; as the willow wilts before the other three species, so Joseph died before his brethren.
>
> Another explanation: *Hadar* symbolizes Sarah, whom the Holy One, blessed be God, honored her (*hidderah*) with good old age; as it says, "Now Abraham and Sarah were old" (Gen. 18:11). "Branches (*kappot*) of palm trees" symbolizes Rebecca; just as the palm tree contains edible fruit as well as prickles, so Rebecca brought forth a righteous man (Jacob) and a wicked one (Esau). "And boughs of thick trees" symbolizes Leah; just as the myrtle is crowded with leaves so was Leah crowded with children. "And willows of the brook" symbolizes Rachel; as the willow wilts before the other three species, so Rachel died before her sister.
>
> (Leviticus Rabbah 30:10)

On Sukkot, all four species are brought together for a blessing. It is as if we need to bring together all the people from our past before we can truly live in the present. Particular individuals and their unique stories, are our keys to survival and strength. Their successes and failures, their lives and their deaths: all these are essential to who we are.

In the twelfth century, a convert named Ovadiah wrote to Maimonides, a great rabbinic sage, with a question. "Can I praise the God and God of my ancestors, Abraham, Isaac, and Jacob," he inquired, "even though I have come to Judaism born of others?" Maimonides' answer was a resounding yes. Like Ovadiah, I came to realize that becoming a Jew meant claiming the biblical ancestors as my own. Moreover, it occurred to me that the people I had actually come from were not so different than the ushpizin of old. After all, if the characters on Ben Yehudah Street could all look so different from each other and yet be part of the same tradition, perhaps there was room for mine.

Ushpizin at the Thanksgiving Table
(Be Careful Passing the Gravy)

In Judaism, Sukkot is the time when the stories of our ancestors are told. In my family growing up, as in so many other American families, those stories were told at Thanksgiving.

Preparing for Thanksgiving was a grand production in my home. By the time I was old enough to see over the table, I was conscripted for duty beginning at daybreak on Thanksgiving. My responsibilities included opening cans of shiny black olives big enough to fit over fingers, and plastic wrapping everything, for the first three of what could easily hit five or seven courses. Years later, when Lisa came for her first Thanksgiving dinner and was eager to please, she asked for seconds on the first course, thinking it was the only one.

Little did she know. Like any sacred meal, this one was ripe with symbols, historical metaphors, and overfeeding. Any guests invited to our Thanksgiving would have had a similar experience to what it feels like to leave a first seder: with a sense that there was a lot more to learn, and also with a sense of bloating.

As children, my brother and I would help set up the plates, while we joined the cats in swiping the condiments: a pickle here, a piece of antipasto there. We were adept at restoring the pillaged items to a newly hollowed-out glory. When my grandparents still lived in the apartment upstairs, my brother and I were also the last-minute dumb waiters shuttling food between floors of the house. My grandfather was never to be trusted with hot food items and gravity.

The magic of Thanksgiving with my family required hours of stress and preparation. My mother's spiraling anxiety was the fuel that propelled the day forward. At some point, she would realize that an essential ingredient had been forgotten. My father would have to rush to the store— chauffeured of course, because he never learned how to drive.

After hours of preparation, we were not permitted to sit down. There was always more food to be wrapped—not to mention the furniture. Before the guests arrived, the whole house was covered with plastic. The museum-like living room, its chairs, and its couches, seemed wrapped like the food in plasticized anticipation. We were forbidden to touch anything. The penultimate moments before the guests arrived felt like a bus about to plunge off the side of a steep cliff; a very fine balance was needed to avert disaster. The wine and scotch helped.

The seating was difficult, even though the regulars all had their spots. If you brought a guest, they were your responsibility. The wild cards were the family friends who, on the surface, could be seated next to other family members on the basis of creed or ethnicity, but even this was unpredictable.

Our family friends Ruth and Hy, for example, should have been a simple seating assignment. They were Jewish, so it would have made sense to my grandmother to seat them next to my aunt's gentle and well-mannered Jewish husband Harvey. We were all a bit surprised at the chair fight that almost ensued. Ruth and Hy were staunch Republican Jews. They had no children and lots of money and free time on their hands—which they spent liberally on lobbyists for the Republican Party. Hy was a podiatrist for Richard Nixon. When, as a little girl, I asked him what it was like, one would think by his response that he was a neurosurgeon, or a chief of staff at a major hospital, claiming he knew everything about medicine. The only thing he would tell me about treating Nixon's feet was: "It was confidential . . . and stinky.") My uncle Harvey, on the other hand, was a Jew from proud Floridian and Democratic stock. He was a union man who worked as a customs official for the government, and he was armed.

Like the sukkah, our home became a temporary dwelling for all. Rather than boughs and branches of wood, the medium was plastic wrap. The long meal was full of food, but more than that, it contained scripted moments of memory, with all of the guests' predictable stories and unpredictable characters. Who would burn the tablecloth? Who would fight over politics? Who would ask for gravy as we all yelled responsively "attached!" or "unattached!" (depending on the construction of the gravy boat currently in use). This ritual response recalled the hot tsunami my aunt caused by coming to the wrong conclusion about the "attached-ness" of the gravy boat, many years before. As the wave of scalding gravy flew across the table directly toward my grandfather, our eyes widened; we witnessed what would become yet another part of the miracle of a holiday that always seemed to have more stories.

My favorite stories, though, always were prompted by the moment in which someone would hold up and wave around the crispy, gnarled turkey ass like the shankbone in the Passover story, and remind us that my late grandfather ate only the part that went over the fence last. These stories invited our ushpizin to the table. Like the ushpizin of old, they included patriarchs, priests and prophets, warriors and kings.

The Birdman of Vermont Street

My maternal grandfather's given name was Angelo, but for reasons no one remembers, he hated it. The only time I ever heard it used was when he received an award from the music department at my elementary school. I had started off playing the flute. But natural selection had me destined for something bigger—namely, the tenor saxophone. I was the only child tall enough to reach the mouthpiece and muster the necessary wind power. Height being no indicator of strength, however, there was no way I could carry the instrument the three blocks between my house and my school; instead, my grandfather carried it for me. Twice a week we walked together. His facilitation of my musical career did not go unnoticed. The music teachers were grateful for the increased chance of snagging an all-county band spot from the unlikely pairing of a girl with a huge saxophone.

I only knew my grandfather as Poppy, so the music department got his given name from my school records in the nurse's office. There was not a dry eye at the awards assembly after the director described his diligence. My grandfather got a standing ovation and an award, "To Angelo Bellafiore, in Honor of Distinguished Musical Transportation Service." My grandfather was furious. For weeks afterward, he threatened to return the award to the school.

Instead of Angelo, my grandfather was known as Danny, a good, generic, American name. But those who really knew him, knew him as the Birdman of Vermont Street.

Pigeons raised in rooftop coops were a familiar sight in my grandfather's East New York neighborhood. Raising pigeons was a source of male bonding, and the sport of local kings. Night games watching the Dodgers were eschewed in favor of setting a host of pigeons loose into the twilight air like a climbing feathered vortex. Much time was spent discussing the particulars of cleaning the tail feathers of your favorite birds, sharing secret additions to their feed, or bragging to your buddies about how fast your pigeons could fly.

The men would wait patiently for the flock of birds to return, and dozens never did. War stories about carrier pigeons trained to cross enemy German lines with classified information were shared with much reverence and drama. Like their human friends, many birds went off into battles that took them far from home. Only the few and the brave would ever return. In this Brooklyn neighborhood of proud Italian Americans, even the birds were patriots and fighters.

One of the men with whom my grandfather raised pigeons was Domenic, his neighbor from across the hall. Whatever they discussed over those birds, the friendship formed on these nights developed into bonds of family. When my grandmother hemorrhaged after giving birth to my mother, she needed to be hospitalized for months. Knowing that there was no way her husband could take care of a newborn, my grandmother entrusted the infant to Domenic and his wife, Betty. Although Domenic and Betty did not yet have children of their own, my grandmother knew that her baby would be safe in their hands. The infant stayed with them until my grandmother was strong enough to care for her. This sealed the friendship forever, and the couple were always known to me as Uncle Domenic and Aunt Betty.

Uncle Domenic had served as a marine during World War II, and he was the embodiment of everything that was good about the service. He was a beautiful and powerful man, and even though I knew him when he was old I could see the strength coursing through the veins in his arms. Still, something in him was broken. He had been stationed in Germany at the end of the war, and his outfit liberated Dora-Nordhausen. He gleefully spoke of finding SS soldiers hiding in the forest and shooting them in the legs, and throwing the complicit guards into the mass graves. They were left there for a few hours, before being shot to death, to think about what they had done. He saw his role as bringing a measure of justice to a situation in which horrific injustices had been perpetrated.

Domenic also stole things. He shipped home boxes upon boxes of Nazi memorabilia, taken from the people he had captured in the camps. Once, I asked him why he creatively acquired so many things from his time in Germany. His face lost its perpetual smile, and he told me that he took them because he knew that no one would believe him and that the world needed to know what had happened. Near the end of his life, he gave me a set of photographs that he had refused to ever part with. With his permission, I sent them to Yad Vashem, where they became part of the largest collection of Holocaust-related material in existence. He was incredibly grateful for the assurance that what he had borne witness to would not be forgotten.

When my grandfather and Uncle Domenic moved their families out of East New York, both families went to Long Island. My family moved to Nassau County, and Domenic and Betty moved even farther east, to the farmland of Suffolk County. Coincidentally, Uncle Domenic lived next to a *shmurah* matzah field, where wheat is grown and harvested for hand-made matzah, the flatbread eaten on Passover. Every year, for a few days, dozens of men in black Chasidic garb came with large black bags to harvest the wheat by hand. My Uncle Domenic had spent years under the assumption that the men were Amish. He knew nothing about Judaism, and knew very few Jews. There is no doubt that he knew more about pigeons. But he knew what it meant to be a human being, to fight for what was right, and leave a legacy for those yet to come.

Domenic continued to raise carrier pigeons. Whenever they visited our home, he would bring Bertha and Sammy along, and we would attach small notes to their feet. About a week later, I would get the note back in the mail. As a child, I was fascinated by these pigeons. Uncle Domenic even taught me to look at their toes and see how each had different nail colors based on the coloration of their feathers: sometimes, multicolored pigeons had three or four different colors of claws. This gave me a deep and enduring appreciation for the so-called sky rats common in New York City. Rather than loathe them, I love looking at their odd movements, multicolored toes, and beautiful plumage. Uncle Domenic taught me to appreciate these small things. In doing so, he taught me about the beauty that can be found in difference, and the value of each and every life.

For my Uncle Domenic, pigeons were everything, but my grandfather's interests were more diverse. He had many avian companions, but a tiny white parakeet, Pretty Boy, was his favorite. His job as a U.S. Customs officer at Kennedy Airport gave him ample opportunity for many things to literally fly his way. Some nights it was imported perfumes and African decorative art that followed him home. One night, it was the small bird my family would come to revere as Pretty Boy.

Pretty Boy was an Oliver Twist with feathers. My grandfather taught him how to pickpocket coins and bills, honing Pretty Boy's primal affinity for all things shiny and crinkly. The bird was such an adept student that he would break into family piggy banks and drop coins one by one onto the floor, all for the sheer joy of hearing the clink of change on the tiles or the crisp crunch of bills under his claws. Despite having their savings raided by Pretty Boy on a daily basis, my mother and aunt warmed to him, once they realized they could dress him up in doll outfits.

Everyone loved Pretty Boy. He may have been a kleptomaniac, but he had redeeming qualities. For my grandfather, Pretty Boy was the son he never had: dashing and entertaining, with a good work ethic and a head for money. Pretty Boy entered the realm of family legend when he pulled a hundred-dollar bill out of the pocket of the candy store owner next door, a stubby and crude man with a perpetual half-smoked cigar in his mouth. Not only was Pretty Boy's behavior lucrative, but it showed good moral judgment. The candy store owner was known for pinching my aunt and my mother's cheeks to the point of physical abuse, and my family felt that quiet retribution from above was called for. Pretty Boy was smart enough to target a person with a thick wad of cash and lousy character. What more could any birdman ask?

Pretty Boy set the bar very high for the next bird who came my grandfather's way: the Thanksgiving grand prize in a raffle at the local Italian American Social Club on Rockaway Avenue. Pretty Boy's successor in the annals of Bellafiore family history also was a white bird. This one, however, was a massive tom turkey, very much alive. With its snowy white feathers and a three-foot wingspan, it was an angelic creature full of piss and vinegar. The stuffing was yet to come.

My grandfather crossed the threshold proudly, like a caveman who had just bagged a mammoth. The turkey was in a sleeper-hold under his arm, and was no doubt less enthusiastic. My grandfather initially had the upper hand in this wrestling match pitting Angelo against the avian angel. My mother, who was six at the time, and her younger sister were very excited to see the turkey. Other than Pretty Boy, few animals that entered their home had lasted. My grandmother had tried to keep two turtles, Myrtle and Byrtle; one boiled to death when its tank was accidentally left on the heater, and the other was frozen when my grandmother brought it outside to keep her company one winter day while she hung out the wash. Their fates were reminiscent of the opening line of a poem by Robert Frost, in which some predict the world will end in fire, others in ice. Myrtle and Byrtle were sorry exemplars of both opinions. The one mammal that had made it through the door had also had an abbreviated tenure: Fritzy, a small dachshund, wet the floor once and was promptly fitted with a set of cement booties and sent out for a swim.

The turkey, by contrast, looked more continent than the dachshund and more sturdy than the turtles. Maybe, my mother and her sister thought excitedly, this pet would be the one that would last. For them, the turkey's arrival promised a new companion. My grandmother knew better.

As far as my grandfather was concerned, he had completed his job as the hunter by winning the turkey. Once escorted safely into his home, the turkey fell into the domain of women's work. My grandmother was a petite and peaceful woman, and she was no match for the turkey. She didn't know what to do, and she refused to kill it; the task would have to be my grandfather's.

In the tightly enclosed space of my grandmother's kitchen, the turkey attempted a last flight. My grandfather, furious at having to do this job, went with his instincts: he attacked the turkey as he would a human opponent, rather than as a meal. He took out his favorite knife, a giant Italian stiletto, always perfectly balanced and sharp. He raised his arm and stabbed the turkey in the neck.

Whatever the stiletto's intended use, it was not the best tool for killing a turkey. The turkey's head was only partially severed. Blood pumping from its neck rhythmically, like a fast sprinkler, the bird did a death lap around the shiny white tiles of the meticulously clean 1950s kitchen. My mother and her sister huddled under the kitchen table, traumatized and screaming. My grandmother simply passed out. Then, giving chase, my grandfather finished the job.

When my grandmother regained consciousness, she was left to defeather, drain, and cook the dead monstrosity in her small oven. Years later, she would liken this task to using an Easy-Bake oven to make a wedding cake. My mother and aunt recall that it was the most succulent and delicious turkey they had ever enjoyed.

Truly, fear opens the heart and tenderizes the soul.

Long after my grandfather died, I was working my way through rabbinical school by tutoring math and science all over Long Island. One particular job took me to a wealthy North Shore neighborhood to help a family whose child had once again failed Earth Science. Three mornings a week, I trekked to their estate and taught their son the subtleties of igneous, sedimentary, and metamorphic rocks. I dreaded he would inevitably fail in a blaze of glory. Adding insult to injury, after each session, I would be bullied by a gang of tom turkeys that roamed outside the main house. I never realized how big turkeys were in real life, or how ugly their heads. They looked like small vultures as they circled me like a gang from a Brando movie. The ones on my Thanksgiving table, redolent in herb stuffing, had never seemed threatening.

One morning, the turkeys finally made their move. I got pecked about seven times, enough to make my legs bleed though my jeans. I smacked one turkey with a Barron's guide, but it only infuriated the rest. Too embarrassed to admit that I had just been assaulted by poultry, I drove away defeated, determined to have an extra helping of turkey when the season approached, and thinking of my grandfather.

Despite having vanquished the turkey, my grandfather was not a lucky man. He was an orphan by age five, left to the sporadic care of his three older siblings. Beer and sugar water were considered food groups, and his legs bowed from rickets. After a few years as a child laborer in his older brother's furniture store, he ran away and lived on the street, ejected into independence as a prematurely emancipated minor. What he did between then and the time he met my grandmother is the stuff of hushed family lore. By the time he was a teenager, he was already screen-legend handsome with a penchant for moral relativism that everyone seemed to love.

Ever the optimist, he considered whatever he had in his pockets lucky. A coin was lucky simply by virtue of the fact that it was in one's own pocket and not in someone else's. He carried a *mano carnuto*, a small red plastic hand with two fingers extended to resemble horns, at all times. He spent hours teaching me and my brother to steal it from one of his pockets and replace it in another without him noticing. It was not enough to simply pull it; we had to return it to him as well. Upon discovering the switch, he would feign a roar and pretend to pitch a loud fit. For us this was a great source of amusement, for him a great source of pride. It was important to him that we were able to take care of ourselves by any means necessary. Ever the experiential teacher, he wanted us to count pickpocketing among our blossoming talents. In his own way, he was sharing a crucial survival skill. On Grandparents' Day in elementary school, the other children spoke about baking pies and going shopping. I invented similar domesticated scenarios, figuring I should probably keep my cherished memories of petty larceny to myself. Years later, when I first saw a *yad*, the pointer with a carved hand at the end used for reading Torah, it was my grandfather's mano carnuto that came incongruously to mind.

When I was a little girl, my grandfather took me to see the horses at Belmont. We sat in the stands together, enjoying a snack while he played the ponies. After the races, we went to meet the jockeys. They were about my height, but we were clearly traveling in opposite directions on the growth chart. He charmed them into letting me give a winning horse a carrot. Even though he never won, he seemed pleased with the outcomes. I didn't ask any questions, I only knew that my grandfather made his own luck. Making luck ran in the family. My grandfather's eldest sister, and last surviving sibling, was our Aunt Sylvie. Her spells and medicinal rituals hailed from the rural black hills of Sicily, and were a source of embarrassment to the Italian Catholics in my family.

Aunt Sylvie fell into the "Sith Lord" category of relatives. Appearances were deceiving. Her Yoda-like posture and broken English suggested a harmless sweet old lady, but in reality, she was a seething dark Emperor in disposition and dentition. She despised all of us for reasons long forgotten—or long repressed. My family collectively dreaded going to her house, and only did so, a few times a year, out of deference and fear of my grandfather.

The many crucifixes in Aunt Sylvie's Ozone Park home made Jesus look like a biology dissection. His skin was painfully stretched over a bloodied skeletal body with a seemingly negative body mass index. This was not a pretty body of Christ. I wondered what had happened to the buff, perky, blond Jesus from the storybooks at church. Was it cancer? Was there a tragic accident we had just not gotten to yet in Sunday School? Surely, if God had let this happen to His son, I worried, the rest of us were toast. The other icons around Aunt Sylvie's home did not fare much better; an assortment of saintly ceramic murder victims riddled with arrows and swords decorated the dusty shelves.

"Don't look her in the eye and don't let her throw anything on you," my grandmother would say. "Hand over anything she gives you, change your clothes and shower as soon as you get home. You should probably pray, too." We did not dare ridicule Aunt Sylvie's beliefs, however arcane, and we were all genuinely scared. Her magic worked in large part because she believed that it worked. Chicken bones and all, she was absolutely irony-free. Gnarled by age and anger, her powers of suggestion were still tremendous. Looking back, this woman was as close to being clergy as anyone in my family had ever come, aside from the Native American chief and shaman who had married my grandfather's sister Tilly, a few generations back.

"Never," my grandmother would sternly instruct us, "*never* look in the back of her fridge." If only I had taken this sage advice. On one visit, Aunt Sylvie instructed me to go get salami to make a sandwich. As I took the overly fragrant sandwich meat from the refrigerator, I accidentally glanced behind it, forgetting my grandmother's warnings until it was too late. A jar of inhuman eyes looked back. The yellowing orbs and their strings of attached tissue bobbed in a greenish, viscous fluid. I was disgusted but, strangely, not surprised. In the parts of Sicily that my Aunt Sylvie came from, animals were used fully; what wasn't food was a potential pharmaceutical. There was no medicine cabinet; there was only the fridge.

When she first met my grandfather, my grandmother had vainly attempted to befriend her future sister-in-law for the sake of self-preservation. Even then, Sylvie was the standard bearer of superstition and purveyor of family fortunes, despite having been both abandoned by her husband and hit by a bus in the span of a year. My grandmother felt a deep sense of pity for Sylvie's misfortunes, perhaps because she herself had been hit by a trolley car, her sister hit by a bus, and her father killed by a train. Neither lithe nor lucky, my mother's family now has a healthy fear of public transportation; suburban living with its large garages, safety innovations, and righteous indignation at the prospect of walking or taking a bus has added years to our lives.

One snowy day a few years ago, this family tradition of misfortune with moving vehicles flashed through my mind when my car was lifted off the ground by a massive tour bus making an illegal right turn from the middle lane in front of Madison Square Garden. My tiny Honda was pushed up on two wheels and dragged into the main intersection. Looking up into the tinted bus windows, much closer than they should have been, I saw the contorted faces of screaming retirees, who had been en route to Atlantic City and hadn't counted on someone else's bad luck. The action also interrupted a crowd of Tibetan protesters in saffron robes, who were chanting peace songs but scattered to make way for the carnage. My passenger, a rabbinical student, got out of the car when it stopped and eagerly approached the Tibetans, hoping her request that they be witnesses to our automotive mauling would lead to a productive interfaith moment. Instead, the saffron robes were quickly tucked away and their owners blended into the crowd, willing to bear witness to genocide but not to a car accident. As the crowd of Tibetan protesters scattered, I wanted to roll down my window and reassure them: "Don't worry, it's not about you. My family has issues with things that move."

The last time we visited her, Aunt Sylvie's behavior had become increasingly erratic. "Wayva-tooda-plaina, wayva-tooda-plaina," she mumbled repeatedly under her breath. Her eyes were closed tightly, as if she was lost in prayer. At first, we politely ignored the incomprehensible murmuring as best we could. Once the swaying and screaming kicked in, though, more concern was warranted.

"Wayva-tooda-plaina! Wayva-tooda-plaina!" Her voice grew louder, and she rocked back and forth. We gathered in her kitchen, sure that she had finally lost it. As her shouting and gyrations hit a fever pitch, we wondered whether she was crying out for a final divine reprieve or putting a hex on us yet again. The ground began to shake.

"Wayva-tooda-plaina!" she screamed once more, now gesturing wildly at the window. Had she just called down the apocalypse? Was Jesus finally coming back *exactly* as pissed off as she always told us he would be?

We hit the floor screaming as the dirty underbelly of an ascending 747 buzzed her Ozone Park apartment. She waved to the plane, just as she had been instructing us to do, and cackled at us for the better part of an hour. My Uncle Joey was not the only one with incontinence issues that day.

The sibling resemblance between Aunt Sylvie and my grandfather was uncanny, even though they looked nothing alike. Both were terrifying in their own ways to everyone they knew. Neither had a problem calling the powers of heaven or hell to protect themselves, and occasionally their family.

While my Aunt Sylvie relied on spells and incantations, my grandfather was somewhat more practical. He wore knives as other people wore accessories or clothes. He once showed me the definition of a sharp blade: he took out the knife he was wearing that day and demonstrated how it could cut through paper. When I found his knives in a cigar box after his death, they were still razor sharp. He had stones and mineral oils for sharpening, and he hated that my father used the guy who came to sharpen things in a truck. Every other week, what looked like an ice cream truck full of knives rang its way down the block. It always seemed to drive a little faster than the embarrassed husbands who would chase it with dull knives instead of sharpening them themselves.

My grandfather always had the right knife to match the occasion. While some men reveled in the chivalry of "Do you need a light?" he was tickled, by any opportunity to respond to "I can't open this," in which case the seven-inch switchblade would come out. At Christmas, he had his opening knife for presents. When he went to walk the dog, he had one to whittle sticks while he was waiting for the dog to do its business. He had two knives for opening letters, one for those from people he liked and one for those from people he didn't; they looked exactly the same. He also had a skinner, which he used to skin the squirrels he shot, with a Daisy BB gun, in the front yard from his second-floor window.

The BB gun had many uses. My grandfather would take aim from this second floor, suburban window, shooting holes in the tires of anyone who dared park in front of our house. One day, I came home to see a group of people gathered outside, trying to determine where the shots had come from. All of a sudden, everyone turned around and looked up at his window, and all you could see was him looking out and then ducking back in. There was a collective realization of the shots' origin, but also that there would be no justice that day. Very rarely did people park in front of our house after that. Everyone was too scared of my grandfather to go to the police; it was never spoken of again.

Years later, a week before my grandfather died, I came across one of the strange red mano carnuto charms in his desk. As a child, I had debated the wisdom of poking at the devil in any fashion, and my questions on the topic were stifled before I could get them out. I knew I would not have many more chances to ask grandfather about it. When I brought the charm to his bedside, I asked him about its significance, and I expected the kind of cautionary religious response his sister would have offered. His six-foot-three frame was withered from lung cancer, and the amusement from my question made him cough and wheeze. He caught his breath, pulled me close, and whispered into my ear, "When you are in a fight, always go for the eyes first so they never see you coming." It was the last time I ever heard him laugh.

The Blessing of Our Ancestors: As Many as the Stars in the Sky

Whether a sukkah is in America or Israel, when you look up on a clear night, you can see the stars through the skhakh. My Israeli intruder had the right idea: palm fronds make a perfect covering, despite the phobia of open windows and partial nudity that has stayed with me ever since.

Like fingers over a child's eyes as she peeks at a surprise, the skhakh gives the sky a frame and makes us notice the stars. The stars in turn call to mind the first of the ushpizin, Abraham, who began the journey. God's blessing to Abraham is that his descendants should become as many as the stars of the sky. Some of those descendants came into this world Jewish by birth, and others of us have found our own paths. As a convert to Judaism, my Hebrew name—Yonah bat Avraham v'Sarah—identifies me as a child of Abraham and Sarah; the names of my chosen ancestors are taken as part of my own. This is the name with which I was ordained as a rabbi, and with which I am called up to the Torah. But I also keep the name with which I was born.

A guiding principle for me is that of Rav Kook, the first chief rabbi of the modern State of Israel. Our task as modern Jews, he taught, is "to make the old new, and to make the new holy"—to breathe new life into ancient traditions, and to make sure our innovations were sacred. We are meant to keep what we have been given, and to transform it. This is what I try to do with the stories I inherit from my family, as well as with those I inherit from Jewish tradition.

The ancestral guests I invite into the sukkah, both ancient and modern, together, light my way. By no means perfect, they were wanderers: morally complicated people who were larger than life. I remember them for their strength, their decency, and their humanity—even when little was shown them. I remember them for their honest and sometimes bloody wrestling with all the vicissitudes of life.

Instead of a mano carnuto, my hand holds a yad. Still, I share the imperative to protect those I love, even though I know that any shelter we give each other is ultimately as temporary as the sukkah. I have kept my grandfather's knife collection. It reminds me of a time when I felt protected from anything and anyone in the world. To many, my grandfather was a rough, violent man, but to me he was a guarantor of safety. I will never have the pleasure of inviting my grandparents or their friends over for a meal in my sukkah. Instead, I rely on the ushpizin to surround me with their memory. As a Jew, I do not subscribe to the dualist notion of heaven and hell. I just know my grandfather is somewhere good, though not nearly as good as the place where my grandmother is, silently stabbing some bastard who looked at him crooked. I miss them so much.

That moment of discovery on Ben Yehudah Street will accompany me wherever my own wanderings take me, along with the family I have made. My own private ushpizin is filled with lifetimes that will never again overlap. I think of Thanksgivings long past, with everyone around the table. They are all in rare form and the meal never ends. I have so many new stories to tell them, and so many wonderful people for them to meet. The Talmud speaks of a messianic banquet where the leviathan, the phoenix, and the behemoth will be served. Perhaps at that eschatological time, we will all sit around the table, eat the flesh of legendary monsters, and laugh together once more.

6

Chanukah

Miller Light

> The House of Shammai maintain: On the first day eight lights are lit and thereafter they are gradually reduced; but the House of Hillel say: On the first day one is lit and thereafter they are progressively increased. . . . The House of Hillel's reason is that we increase in [matters of] sanctity but do not reduce.
>
> —Babylonian Talmud, Shabbat 21b

The scent of singed cat made an appearance in our home the night the Christmas tree went up. The ornaments were placed carefully on the tree, and my father's favorite music, the Christmas collection of the Germanic boysinger Heintje, was set on a loop to play through the night. My father's penchant for Teutonic music was given free rein over the holidays. We all quietly thanked God that Abba never made a Christmas album.

Because my parents bought their tree late in the season to save money, there were two basic models left to choose from. There was the supermodel tree, which looked emaciated and dropped its needles as if it had just come off a bulimic bender at Fashion Week. Then, there was the size-queen tree, a more frequent choice. This beast of a tree took up half the living room. Whatever the shape, the scent was the same. The tree made the whole living room smell like

Bed Bath & Beyond right after Thanksgiving. It's a particular potpourri that at once evokes notes of pine and nutmeg, subtly undercut by the stench of drunken relatives.

That particular year, we had the Jeff Stryker model. After the tree was well hung with balls, the humans of the house went to bed. But for the cats, the night was just beginning. After hours of being taunted by the tree's blinking lights, our youngest and perkiest cat, Miller, gave in to temptation and pounced upon the wires. As Heintje's effeminate voice sang of a silent, holy night, we woke to a loud crackling and electric popping sound, followed by a muffled thump on the opposite wall. After a brief search, the animal was discovered still smoking, his fur puffed like a dynamite Cleopatra Jones afro. His whiskers curled from the electric shock, Miller staggered off like a jittery extra from *Pet Sematary*, and slumped between piles of presents.

The stacks of gifts seemed to get higher every year. My family doesn't drive fancy cars. They don't have ostentatious clothes, and they don't take extravagant vacations. They don't pretend to ski, or know famous people, and true crime novels and *America's Test Kitchen* cookbooks are standard bedside reading. Christmas is the one time of year they like to show off a little. For my father, that meant buying my mother good suits for work, and jewelry from Tiffany's. These special gifts never came on birthdays or anniversaries, but only at Christmastime, when my mother held court. She genuinely enjoyed these little powder-blue-boxed tokens of my father's esteem, and he loved giving them.

At some point in the 1990s, however, everything changed. My mother was buying a card at a ninety-nine-cent store and saw something that would transform our lives forever. It was a Beanie Baby, and its siren song fell upon willing ears. A week later, she returned and bought another, and another. Before anyone realized it, she had a full-on addiction that required hundreds of small plexiglas boxes. The red sign on the door of the room where they are enshrined to this day warns "This Room Is Protected by Beanie Babies—Enter at Your Own Risk." Rows upon rows of beady eyes follow you as you enter the room, pleading: "Play with us! Free us! Cut off our swing tags!"

The collection grew. From the moment of that first purchase, all my mother wanted for Christmas was Beanie Babies. Once my father made his peace with that fact, he went to the ends of the earth to find her the ones that she wanted. We suspect that he is solely responsible for the surge in the Beanie market on eBay in the 1990s. My mother is not an easy woman to please, and the premise of finding something that would make her happy was an opportunity he was not going to pass up. And so Beanie Babies joined the presents under the tree.

Gift-giving would come after dinner on Christmas Eve, which, in true Sicilian fashion, featured twelve kinds of fish to represent the twelve apostles. This seemed like a lot of fish for a family riddled by iodine allergies. Italian tradition generally required seven types of fish, recalling the miracle of the loaves and the fishes; being a sea-faring people, however, Sicilians required twelve. This made sense back in Sicily, where there was ready access to a great abundance and diversity of piscine life, but on Long Island it was more of a stretch. My grandfather would go ocean fishing with hand-wrapped, lacquered fishing poles that he made himself out of bamboo. They were works of art, and each one bore his signature. He could not, however, fish for Christmas dinner in December. Instead, my mother would make a pilgrimage to her fishmonger, far away on on Point Lookout, where the fish came fresh off the docks. She and the other Italians would complain, while standing on line, asking themselves and each other why they kept this tradition year after year: "Why can't we just buy Christmas candy like everybody else?" they would ask. "Why do we have to get the damn fish?" Sitting at the table Christmas Eve, I too wondered, albeit less vocally and with less colorful language, why we had this tradition.

Other concerns remained. Once the major species of seafood had been accounted for, it was pretty much downhill. You quickly started getting into the dregs of creamed fish, eel, and salt-preserved critters that smelled like briny death. Somehow, no one noticed the irony that the apostles could not have eaten at least seven of the twelve kinds of fish we could get. Eel was not on the menu for a first-century Jew. Unfortunately for me, it was on ours, and it had all of the consistency and flavor of the inner tube of a bicycle.

We never spoke about the spiritual symbolism of food. Like the unexplained lamb on Easter, these fish just seemed to be something else on the table that nobody ate. When I asked my parents what the fish on Christmas Eve were for, they surmised that the concept of "apostles as fishers of men" would be too complicated for my young mind. They told me instead that the twelve kinds of fish were there to honor the twelve people who kept Jesus company. My only prior model for a charismatic figure surrounded by friends was my Disney pillowcase, featuring Snow White and the seven dwarves; Snow White thus became not just angelic but positively messianic in my mind, and Sleepy, Dopey, Sneezy, et al. were her holy posse. Upon watching a documentary about Leonardo da Vinci's *Last Supper* on PBS with my grandmother, I was further convinced that the apostles were dwarves. They weren't sitting at the table; they were standing—and short. In the painting, Jesus was looking downward politely, just as my brother and I were told to do upon encountering someone different from ourselves: "Don't stare!" my mother would say in a stage whisper, accompanied by an excruciating pinch. I vividly remember my first encounter with "the pinch." From the stroller, I had shouted excitedly, "Mommy, Mommy! It's Gordon from *Sesame Street*!" when we passed a tall, bald, black man on Jamaica Avenue in Hollis, Queens. I wondered whether Jesus' mother also gave him a death pinch on the arm to make sure he behaved.

When the time finally came to give out the gifts on Christmas Eve, the family gathered in the shadow of the tree. My mother was the master of ceremonies, announcing, with Remy Martin–inspired aplomb, the names of the giver and recipient of each gift, as written on the gift tag. Some, like my aunt and uncle, had their own terms of endearment: "To Cookie Puss from Fudgie the Whale," "To Hot Lips from Cold Hands," and the classic "To Long Neck from No Neck." Most, though, were more straightforward. At some point, my mother must have gotten tired of reading "From Mom and Dad," so other household members were recruited. Once the standard family gifts were doled out, things got a bit more creative: "To Andrea from Zippy 2 the Hamster" and "To Todd Alan from the Cats."

I found this idea enchanting. As a child, I imagined the pets sneaking spare change from the laundry over the course of the year, then running off together like the animals in *The Incredible Journey*, racing toward the mall. I had it all figured out: after buying the gifts, they would commandeer a taxi home, using an old gas bill to tell the driver their address; they would arrive home with gifts precariously balanced on their backs, and make a break for the basement; there, they would quickly wrap the goods and hide them for the upcoming holiday. The only elusive detail was how they wrote the gift tags.

Cats giving presents: that was more plausible than other aspects of this holiday. I didn't want to debunk Christmas. Rather, I just wanted cold hard evidence that would convince me that my parents were not lying to me. I hoped against hope that the man in the red suit and white beard who looked suspiciously like my father truly was an arctic philanthropist with a lot of frequent flyer miles. Surely Santa, like my father, could also have taken to wearing Royall Bay Rhum cologne. More than anything, I wanted to believe in the magic of the season. But too many things didn't make sense, and I grew tired of the constant suspension of reality that masked itself as holiday cheer.

When I was five, I began to ask for proof: specifically, a Polaroid photograph of Rudolph the Red-Nosed Reindeer. I knew that a photo of Santa could easily be staged. But Rudolph was a different story. I wanted to see Rudolph, the deer with the horns and the fur and the glowing nose. I didn't need to see proof of him flying, but I did want to see that nose.

Every year, when Santa was leaving our house, my mother pointed to the water tower in the distance, where a red light shone, and told me that it was Rudolph coming to pick Santa up. I made a point of looking outside, the next night, at the same time, only to see that the red light was indeed still there. Either Rudolph had gotten stuck in a holding pattern, or my parents weren't telling the whole truth. Only a photograph could tell me for sure. And it had to be a Polaroid; even at that young age, I had a feeling that photographs could be doctored. I voiced my doubts about the moon-landing early on. The pictures always seemed shady in all the wrong places.

All this blossomed into a broader interest in conspiracy theories. In elementary school, I was already reading the

Warren Commission Report and was fascinated by the details surrounding the assassination of JFK. So I made my demands for evidence very clear. I told my father I wasn't going to do Christmas anymore until I saw a Polaroid of Rudolph with a red nose. The grassy knoll was optional. My bleary-eyed father made a final concerted effort to save Christmas for me. He found an artist whom he commissioned to do a small painting of Rudolph, complete with a bright red nose. In actuality, if he had brought home a regular photograph of an ordinary reindeer, it probably would have sufficed. But when I saw him holding the framed painting, hands shaking ever so slightly as he offered it to his five-year-old skeptic, we both knew that the jig was up. Years later, standing in line at the DMV being told that my forms of identification were insufficient, this moment came back to me. The miniature painting was very sweet, but it simply was not an acceptable form of proof.

All told, my father never had much luck around Christmas. One Christmas Eve, he stayed late at the bank where he worked. Despite the early holiday closing, many people in his area were staying behind to do mutual fund evaluations after the market had closed. My father didn't want to leave until all the staff members had completed their tallies. Out of the goodness of his heart, he spent some time going from party to party in the building while they worked. He came back to his own group's area and went into the bathroom. A well-dressed man was standing next to him at the urinal. My father wished him a Merry Christmas; the man turned around and took out a gun.

"There I am, hanging out," my father now recalls, "and I said to him, 'There are people outside, what if one of them comes in?' 'I'm going to kill you first,' the man replied. That got my attention," says my father. The thief told my father to go into a stall and pass his pants and money underneath the door. More afraid of coming home to my mother without his Christmas bonus than of being shot, my father gave up his pants, but kept the money. He heard someone else coming in—one of his own employees, who was given the same routine, minus the pants. Then the bathroom door opened and closed as the mugger left. After five minutes, my father climbed onto the toilet seat and looked over the divider into the next stall. There he saw the other man, terrified, huddled on the bowl in a fetal position. "You have to go out," my father said to him, "because I don't have any pants." The man eventually collected himself, went out, and brought my father his raincoat. My father, wearing a coat and no pants like a flasher, went down to security, told them about the mugging, and borrowed a pair of pants. When he arrived home that evening with his money and manhood intact, he was met by a variety of responses. My Sicilian grandfather, looking askance at his son-in-law and making stabbing motions with his fork, mumbled curses under his breath: "*Gavone*, I'd have gutted the bastard like a fish with my bare hands for even talking to me in a bathroom." For me, the event was reinforcement of a belief that my father was like James Bond—traveling the world, doing work he couldn't explain, meeting interesting people, and always having adventures. For my mother, it reinforced a different belief: buying suits with two sets of pants for ninety dollars was the way to go, instead of the four-hundred-dollar suit from Barneys, the sole pair of pants of which my father had just lost. "They never stole the other pants," she said. Years later, when my father ruined another perfectly good pair of pants by being shot in the ass on the streets of Brooklyn, my mother shared similar wisdom.

Rudolph was the first mythical figure to go. Next came the Tooth Fairy. In second grade, I set up a mint-dental-floss trap in my bedroom, reasoning that I would both trip the intruder and be able to verify my findings by the minty scent left on his or her shoes. I put two nails into the doorframe and strung the dental floss across the bottom. The fairy trap was an immediate success. "Shit!" my mother exclaimed as she tripped over the floss. The coins she held went flying across the room. "Where did those damned quarters go?" Even if she hadn't tripped, the tip of her lit cigarette was a dead giveaway. I certainly wasn't about to believe in a Tooth Fairy who smoked. I feigned sleep, mostly because I wanted the money. More money meant more candy, and fewer teeth meant less room for cavities. It was a perfect combination.

After both the Tooth Fairy and Rudolph had been busted, my parents had a lot at stake with the Easter Bunny. We never did Easter egg hunts, because they wisely did not want me and my brother rummaging through their belongings. Instead, they—or, rather, the Easter Bunny—left presents on the kitchen table. My brother and I would stay up late and wait until we saw the glow of my mother's cigarette disappear. When the coast was clear, we would tiptoe to the table, unwrap our presents, play with them, and rewrap them for the morning. When morning came, eager to provide a distraction from our sloppy efforts at repackaging, we would quickly direct our parents' attention to the decorated Easter eggs or the half-eaten carrots scattered on top of the table. My parents had left the carrots there the night before, as a present for the Easter Bunny, and the bite marks were presented to us as evidence of his visit. Ever the scientist, I took a carrot with me to the local library, found the forensic books on animal bites, and quickly established that the dentition of a human being, not a bunny, had been at work. I considered taking the carrot to my dentist for further verification, but figured he would also be in on the hoax. Although, looking back, if I had asked Dr. David Horowitz about the Easter Bunny, he might well have told me the truth.

After my rejection of the trinity of Rudolph, the Tooth Fairy, and the Easter Bunny, Jesus didn't stand a chance. Years later, when I told my parents I was becoming a Jew, the only response they gave was a brief expression of relief. Since I had already told them I was gay, they said, "At least you're returning to God." Six months later, I told them I was going to become a rabbi instead of a doctor. My mother said that I was "flushing a perfectly good medical career down the crapper." But by that point, I could have told them that I was going to become a Tibetan nun in the Himalayas and they wouldn't have blinked.

In college, I was immediately attracted to Judaism as a religion that encouraged children to ask questions, not simply to repeat answers. The miracles found within Judaism also seemed to have a more plausible feel. Specifically, the miracles of Chanukah at least seemed within the realm of possibility. The Jewish people have had no shortage of military miracles over the millennia, but a miracle involving *oil*? This was in the category of miracles involving household products, which made much more sense to me. We have all experienced them: the toilet paper that lasted three weeks; the house plant that would not die; the box of tampons that always had one more . . . not to mention the self-cleaning litter box. Although, for that last one, we discovered that the miracle worker was actually the dog, caught red-pawed, foot-first in the cat box, with a beard of cat litter still hanging from his chin. So much for miracles, in that case.

Perhaps it is good that people keep asking questions about Hanukkah and what its miracle means. In every generation, it seems to change. For the ancient rabbis, the question was *Mai Chanukah?* "What is Chanukah?" as if no previous version of the story existed, giving them the opportunity to tell it anew. Like my mother, they rewrote history.

And so they took a popular, military holiday that had been left out of the biblical canon, and they put God into the story. They knew that people needed a celebration with a sound-and-light show and good food, and they found a way to make it holy. For modern Jews, it has become a Yuletide foil pimped out to include eight days of gifts, fire, doughnuts, and chocolate.

It also serves as a morality tale of assimilation, pluralism, and conflict between Jews. What's not to love?

My parents' table was not a place for such questions. Sex, religion, and politics had always been taboo. It was only when I came out that I discovered that my parents were right-wing Republicans, well before the phrase "compassionate conservative" became a buzzword. I made the mistake of coming out in the summer of 1992, when the Republicans were assembling in full force at their national convention in Houston. I remember the sick feeling in my stomach that turned into full-on nausea, watching my mother cheering Pat Buchanan's speech. She made a weird whooping sound, like an audience member from Arsenio Hall, when Buchanan said that Bill Clinton's idea of foreign policy was limited to breakfast at the International House of Pancakes. I didn't know much about politics, but I did like pancakes, so Clinton had my vote. Besides, I was fast becoming the embodiment of "Rooty Tooty Fresh 'n' Fruity"—sans bacon.

It turned out that my parents had two operating assumptions in life: first, that everyone was a good person until proven otherwise, and, second, that everyone shared their fundamental beliefs. They did acknowledge that there were other religions, as their own union between a Catholic and a Lutheran was seen as an interfaith marriage. In fact, the Catholic Church had refused to officiate at their ceremony, and my mother never forgot it. She sent her children to Lutheran Sunday school, and never set foot in a Catholic church again. The religious circle widened even more when my aunt (who later became a born-again Christian with a flourishing Mary Kay business) married a Jew. But beyond everyone wrapping his "holiday" gifts in blue paper instead of the traditional red, there was little acknowledgment of theological differences. He was even given a blue stocking that hung over the fireplace, with his name applied with love in festive glitter-glue.

Resistance was futile. The culture of the family was to integrate whatever came, and silence was a sign of respect. Any conversation about difference was seen as an insult, and any question perceived as a criticism. When I would point out that I couldn't eat meatballs made with parmesan, my mother would say, "I already left the pork out! Do you think I'm not honoring your tradition? I'm honoring your tradition. I don't understand why you need to insult us by making it an issue. What do you mean, we need to talk about it?" I soon became a vegetarian.

As 1992 came to a close, Christmas drew nearer, and nothing was said. It was expected that I would still come home from college for the holidays, but it seemed as if my parents were going to completely overlook this major shift in my religious, never mind sexual, identity. When I stepped through the door to my home, it was Christmas as usual. I wearily put my bags down and went into the kitchen, where I saw a ratty box from a discount store sitting on the table. "One Menorah" it said, and I stopped dead in my tracks. My mother now insists they had bought it years before, when my Jewish uncle joined the family, but this was the first I had seen of it. To me, the box said "We're going to accept this, and pretend it's the way it has always been." It was a very touching, poignant moment. I knew that this was as good as I was going to get, so I kept the code of silence and went to take a shower. When I came out, the box was empty, foam and packing materials scattered everywhere, as if a present had been ripped open with excitement. The menorah was plugged in at the window by the tree.

There was only one catch: my mother had lit every other light. The ones that weren't solidly lit were blinking. And, to top it all off, she had taken the white bulbs and replaced them with red. She had used blinking Christmas bulbs, because she thought they were more appealing.

"Mom," I asked, "what happened to the menorah?"

"I thought this looked prettier," she replied.

I was hoping that at least the lights would become prettier in ascending order, but that was not to be. Years later, when I saw the movie *The Birdcage*, I thought of this moment. It's the scene where the Nathan Lane character is trying to look straight for his son's fiancée's Republican parents. He manages to put on a suit, and is almost convincing until he crosses his legs and reveals a flash of bright pink socks. "One does want a hint of color," he implores. Over the years, I've taught my mother how to light the menorah correctly—and even that Chanukah and Christmas don't always coincide. But I also needed to realize that she approached her own religious traditions with an eye to aesthetics; in a way, it was a compliment that she applied the same standards to mine.

The first year Lisa shared Christmas with my parents, she was astounded by the mountains of gifts. We went home with our small Honda Civic packed to the point of bursting. "Where on earth," she asked me, "do they think we have room for a rock fountain?" On a deeper level, though, she wondered whether we could help change the experience. "What about the Christmas spirit?" she asked. "Shouldn't we be doing something more meaningful?" She picked up a Heifer International catalogue that had come in the mail. "Look at this. Next year, we could buy a water buffalo in your family's name and change the life of an Asian subsistence farmer! 'Helping Hooves,' the catalogue says. And we would even get a personalized card!"

I was intrigued by the idea, but figured I should run it by a family member first. I decided to start with my born-again Christian aunt, thinking she would be enthusiastic about uniting the spirit of the holiday with charitable activities. "You want to buy a *what*, dear?" she asked. "I just don't know if that would be appreciated, especially if the water buffalo doesn't even stay here in New York. It's important to think locally. After all, Christmas is about giving to those we love, not just those in need."

From then on, we have never left the well-established gift-giving path of scented candles, gift certificates, and liquor. The Beanie Babies remain out of our league.

At the end of the day, we have all concluded that the holidays are not to be toyed with. Lisa and I wanted to show my family the true meaning of Christmas, but we were the unintentional Scrooge. Just as we know the right way to light the menorah, they know the right way to celebrate Christmas. Although our customs are lost on each other after a certain point, we can still sit together at the table. We happily eat our veggie cutlets at family gatherings, as the tasty bugs of the sea are served. My mother is particularly proud of her daughter and daughter-in-law, the rabbis. She has lost life-long friends over my being Jewish and gay, and her support of us is unwavering. History is rewritten to include lines like "I have always been supportive," "Of course I have no problem with that," and, my personal favorite, "What kind of person cuts off their children?" Once the migraine subsides, I can smile. I have to trust that my mother does not carry a picture of our daughters with Santa that she has promised never to take, unlike the prom picture of me with my high school boyfriend that she carried in her wallet for years. And, as for me, I still have the miniature painting of Rudolph that my father gave me, not because it proved anything about Rudolph, or in any way expressed a longing for a faith I never embraced, but because it proved my father's love.

Lisa and I are confident that we are making our own memories, that our daughters really will learn that Ima's family has their holidays and we have ours. When done correctly, Chanukah can be a grease-stained fiasco. The house smells more like a diner than like Bed Bath & Beyond. Everyone seems to have a unique latke recipe and secret ingredients or techniques, whether lemon juice to keep the potatoes from browning, a hair-dryer to make them extra crispy, or the extra flavor of blood from the box grater's assault on someone's knuckles. There's a certain pride of product coming from these very humble potato pancakes that is grander to me than the greatest tree culled from the snowy white hills of Connecticut. At my Chanukah parties, the holiday is recalled, repeated, and transmitted to a younger generation that understands chocolate, fried food, doughnuts, and presents as their portion of a miracle. Like so many other Jewish miracles, this one saw God taking us, yet again, out of an awful situation to one filled with light and joy. What else do children need? The stereotype of Jews enjoying Chinese food and a movie on Christmas, like so many ethnic stereotypes, will never be true for my family. Instead, our experience includes Lisa burning her fingers roasting chestnuts, and a trunk full of presents given with only the best intentions. We are a small family, sitting around that Christmas table, due to both death and disownment, and we're not willing to make it any smaller. For better or worse, I have never felt more like a Jew than when I sit with my family on Christmas day. And when Chanukah and Christmas do coincide, we leave the presents in the trunk when we get home, and run upstairs to light our own menorah. Never have the lights of Chanukah felt more miraculous, and more like freedom.

Miller died just before Chanukah, two days after my grandmother's yahrzeit. His last morning had been uneventful. He followed my mother around the house, and spent time with his favorite feather toy. He was found in a patch of warm afternoon sunlight with the toy wrapped in his paws.

Last December, three years after Miller died, Ariella made a snow globe in art camp. The snow globe had started life as a jar of artichoke hearts, pressed into service by an ambitious art teacher. It was to be held upside down. On the inside of the cap, Ariella had glued a small cougar figurine, surrounded by shiny metallic flakes, suspended in liquid. She had labeled the little sphere, with her six-year old lettering, akin to a kidnapping note, "Cougar Snow Globe." Immediately, I had a vision of a woman of a certain age, poaching her young prey in Aspen. And then I thought of Miller, resplendent under the tree and surrounded by gifts and tinsel once more.

Holidays are quieter now in my parent's home. There is no mention of overseas livestock donations, and the Chanukah lights are as accurate as the bulbs of an electric menorah can be. But in this universal season of light, the image of a cat on fire illuminates us all.

7

Purim

Surprise Endings

For the miracles and for the redemption, for the strong acts and victories, and for the battles which you fought for our ancestors in those days and in our times: In the days of Mordechai and Esther in Shushan the capital, the evil Haman stood against them. He wanted to destroy, kill, and wipe out all the Jews, from children to elderly, babies and women, on one day: the thirteenth day of the twelfth month, the month of Adar, and to plunder them. But You in Your great mercy undermined his plans and confounded his plots, and turned his deeds on his own head, so that he and his sons were hanged on the gallows. For all this may Your name, our Ruler, be blessed and exalted forever and ever.   —*Al HaNissim* Purim prayer

Vashti: *The Persian King Achashverosh's First Wife. The Marriage Ended Violently When She Refused to Do What He Asked.*

The fifth grade assignment seemed simple enough: write a play, make it legible, and be prepared to read it out loud. After a few regrettable efforts, I realized that there were only so many stories a girl could write about angst-ridden unrequited love and the perfunctory flying unicorn.

Having just seen the movie *A Streetcar Named Desire* at the tender age of nine, I was inspired to write an epic drama. I just needed my Stanley and Stella. My parents simply would not do. My father was a quiet man, and my mother would have beaten him to death with a chair if he ever dared to lay a hand on her.

My answer came, literally, from above. My grandfather's room was directly above my own, and my grandparents had loud disagreements at least twice a week. These altercations lasted about half an hour, and they always ended the same way. Yelling would be followed by the crash of a dish against the wall, and then the television would be turned up: end of argument. Fortunately, my grandmother had many dishes.

The casting call was closed.

The only catch was that I had no idea what to write. The limited subject matter of my heavily censored imagination could not do justice to the genre. I craved inspiration and decided to go right to the source. My brother had been given a tape recorder for his birthday, and it was obvious that the creative potential of this gift was wasted on him. I waited a few weeks for him to lose interest, then liberated it for the sake of art. History, I was sure, would judge me kindly. I planted the machine upstairs, deep under cover, in my grand-parents' pantry. There, it recorded the unedited contents of their dinner conversation. A few hours later, I went upstairs with my little book bag and recovered it. I took it into my bedroom, closed the door, put on headphones, and listened to what, to me, was completely A-level material: I knew I had hit the mother lode. I transcribed five handwritten, double-sided pages that included many of the Sicilian swear words that peppered my grandfather's vocabulary.

A week later, my principal called home about the play I had shared with my class. It had been red-flagged for its strong language, violence, and adult themes. On my way to the principal's office for censure, I heard yelling from the teacher's lounge. As I approached the door, I recognized the familiar lines: "Son of a bitch, if you don't get me a beer, Sally, I will break your neck"; "Get it yourself, lazy bastard"; "Damn it"—this from my burly gym teacher—"I will choke you 'til you're dead and stick you where no one will ever find you, *butana*." Apparently, the play was a big hit with the faculty. But, where others might have been flattered or embarrassed, I was indignant. I wanted to run into the smoke-filled lounge screaming, "Danny isn't angry, he's a maniac—that's just how he talks. Sally never yells back, she speaks quietly just to piss him off. Get it right, you hacks." Instead, I turned around and continued walking down the long hallway, toward inevitable punishment. There would be no Tony award for me. There was only a concerned lecture from my parents about family privacy, three weeks' solitary confinement without dessert, and the quiet respect of my teachers for years to come.

Esther: *"The Hidden One."* Achashverosh's
Second Wife, Chosen in a Beauty Contest.
She Keeps Her Jewish Identity Hidden from Her King.

Vulcans would have been considered drama queens in my parents' home. No one was permitted to leave evidence of traumas and unresolved issues littered about. *Issues* described magazines, not states of mind. Mental angst had to be tightly folded, origami-style, and jammed either right back into one's "overdramatic" head or, in the case of me and my brother, into one's dresser drawers.

By age seven, my brother's kink was hidden food. We both were embarrassed by the perpetual bologna sandwiches that were central to our brown-bag lunches. Although we never ate them, we felt guilty about throwing them away. We could not totally discard our mother's efforts, however Spartan, to keep us fed and clothed. I fed my lunches to the stray animals that followed me to school as if I were the pied piper. This outdoor brood of cats had all originated from a single liberated house cat with big ideas. After years of repression indoors, she wanted to enjoy her freedom. She had an easy admissions policy, and for many years was the sexual equivalent of a community college for cats. Her spawn filled the backyard, and they were always happy for food.

My brother's meals had a different fate. From an early age, he had developed a highly evolved sense of shame. He preferred to cram dozens of lunch bags filled with food into his toy box and the drawers under his bed.

Any odor emanating from my brother's vintage sandwich collection was undetectable. My mother always double-bagged our lunches, and so the rotting cold cuts attracted no attention. They were only discovered months later, after the indoor cats had taken up residence in his room like hippies at Woodstock. Through layers of plastic and piles of dirty clothes, their keen sense of smell had detected an intoxicating aroma. Nothing would move them from their new turf. They brought their toys and other belongings into his room and set up a feline commune, the likes of which my family had never seen. The cats spent entire days in this new locale lounging on their backs, freak-flags flying, swaying back and forth as if they had snorted entire bags of catnip.

In the end, it was this inebriated migration that tipped off my mother. She discovered the cache of sandwiches one morning while we were at school. The remains were excavated, each little biohazard still preserved in its plastic bags. The bologna had curled and discolored but was otherwise intact. The verdant bread had a craggy green complexion, and the mustard, the only natural product in there, was now bright purple. Once the bags were opened, the stink was unimaginable.

We arrived home from school to the stench of rotting meat and bleach. While no one was there to witness my mother's wrath, that fateful day, the cats' faces told the story. They no longer spent their days lounging around in blissed-out comfort. Now, they moved cautiously from room to room in huddled masses, and hid in the hamper for hours at a time. If only my brother could have fit, he would have hid in there, too, to escape our mother's wrath.

My own secrets were much darker. Like many girls, I kept two diaries. My fake diary resided in my night table. This counterfeit diary was regularly updated with predictable musings I had copied out of teen magazines, along with pictures of benign boys. I added stories from "normal" girls I overheard at school. For extra authenticity, a minor effort was made to hide the decoy beneath a Bible.

The real deal was hidden in earnest, behind a panel of drawers inside an old combination safe. Detailed stories of crushes on female teachers and friends, along with bad poetry, were carefully secured from all but my own brooding adolescent eyes. Security concerns around this diary consumed me. I crafted a special tool from a broken screwdriver for the sole purpose of extricating the diary and returning it to its top-secret location. I decided also to use the drawer in front of the hidden panel for additional protection; as a burgeoning preteen lesbian, my wardrobe was already severely deficient, leaving ample drawer space. Taking cues from books I had read about ancient Chinese and Egyptian imperial tombs, I decided to provide my diary with defenses far beyond the decorative lock that accompanied its Hello Kitty cover. I was inspired by ancient divine curses that acted like prehistoric house alarms to deter potential robbers. Whatever clandestine methods I would choose, though, they needed to inspire sufficient terror in the hearts and minds of anyone who might desecrate my diary's resting place. I was determined to make this space impenetrable by any means necessary. I needed more than a place to hide my diary. I needed an army.

The answer came to me with a loud chirp: cicadas. Every summer, these chattering, clunky bugs emerged from the earth and invaded our neighborhood, looking for some hot cicada action. They flew into walls, clogged air conditioner vents, and provided entertainment for the neighborhood cats. Most people greeted their summer arrival with disgust. For me and my best friend Erica, though, this was heaven. Instead of chasing boys or dressing Barbie dolls, we spent our summer days prior to the cicadas' arrival playing Atari games, riding bikes, and swimming in Erica's small pool that never seemed to be chlorinated quite enough. We were thick as thieves, and I had a massive girl crush on her. She was strong and brave, and looked strangely compelling in her Girl Scout uniform. She was the only troop member who refused to wear the mandatory green skirt and had successfully lobbied to wear pants instead. Years later, in high school, she would be an expert marksman and tuba player.

Once the cicadas came, we had our mission. We rode our bikes around town, trying to save any bugs that needed to be flipped over after molting and falling off a branch. For better or worse, we saved hundreds of cicadas each summer. Each was named, and, the next day, we would dutifully return to the scene of the rescue, to see if Tron, Zippy, Devo, and Tootsie were still among the living. If not, we collected their carcasses and buried them in Erica's expansive backyard, in a place we had designated for just this purpose. Keenly aware of our *über-nerd* status, we made signs for our bikes: Cicada Savers Coming Through. Saving these bugs was our windmill. In our travels, I kept a shoebox on the back of my bike that I filled with the empty shells of molting cicadas. I thought they were beautiful. Like clouds or snowflakes, each was unique.

It didn't take long before I figured out that my search for a security device for my diary was over. The cicada shell army would serve perfectly. Over the course of a few days, I placed the shells in the drawer, in front of my diary. Each tiny carapace was arranged in an alternating feet-up and feet-down pattern to best catch the sleeve of a potential snoop with its bristly legs. A legion of hundreds of shells lay in wait. Months went by, and to both my great satisfaction and my disappointment, no attempt was made to find my diary.

I had all but forgotten about it when my secret location was discovered. My brother and I were outside playing in the backyard when we heard my mother's screams.

This was not a woman who was easily rattled. She had the strength and fearlessness of John Wayne, only she was significantly more butch. Hearing our mother shriek like a Victorian woman with mice nipping at her toes was terrifying. My brother and I took cover, each assuming that it was our own discovered secrets that had caused the commotion. "She went through my dresser—I'm dead," he said. I knew better: my beastly sentries had done their worst.

My mother ran screaming from the house with dozens of cicada shells still clinging to the sleeves of her sweater. She ran in circles shrieking and swearing, trying in vain to swat the crunchy insect shells off her person. Her horror only increased as the bodies fell away but, enmeshed in her clothing, their crispy legs remained.

The diary was never found, and my mother cut wide swaths around my room. My brother's room continued to be periodically cleansed and purged, but mine remained undisturbed. Rotting meat was no competition for the mental image of hoards of undead insects. Who knew what other secrets my drawers might keep? My long-suffering mother was not about to find out. Appearances were kept up, and the incident was never spoken of again.

Still, this invasion of my privacy was too close for comfort. The season had passed to get more cicada shells, so I had to rethink my security concerns. I realized that my private thoughts could never be safe outside my own mind. Since I was in no way prepared to deal with the repercussions of coming out at such a young age, I destroyed my diary. I burned it in the fall, after the cicadas had long since disappeared.

Conveniently enough, we had a good supply of kindling. Neither my brother or I ever received an allowance, and my Girl Scout cookie sales had been down, so we were perpetually in need of cash. I was saving up for an action figure of the Fonz. We decided to tie together little bundles of sticks with bright, pretty ribbons, and we sold these as kindling up and down the block for five dollars each. One of the neighbors called my mother and asked, "Do you know that your children are out on the street selling sticks?" Mortified, she showed up as we were making a sale, cut the transaction short, and dragged us home. This left us with about thirty dollars—and that convenient stack of extra sticks.

I lit the kindling on the concrete of the local playground, and there I burned my diary, page by page. It felt like euthanasia, more than anything else. I told myself that I was doing this to keep something worse from happening. Like the cicadas, I knew that I needed to wait for the right season to emerge from the earth.

Mordechai: *Esther's Relative. He Foils a Plot Against the King, and Helps Esther Save the Jewish People from Their Enemy, Haman.*

I wanted to be a superhero. More than anything, I wanted to be Superman. It was the mid-seventies, and I was six years old. Superman was my favorite movie, and he was my favorite character. No one looked better than Christopher Reeve in blue tights. I wanted to be bulletproof, just like him, I hoped against hope that I came from a different planet, and I wanted to save the world. I also wanted to fly—and to keep a perfect head of hair. A few years later, my brother and I and our friend Jeannie were perched on top of our garage like three birds on a wire. We had just seen *Superman 2*, and we were having a debate about physics. My brother was convinced that anyone could fly by jumping off something high enough, while I used my experience in having seen the first Superman movie to insist that a cape was essential. We climbed off the roof, snuck into the house, and stole a pillowcase from my mother's linen closet. We climbed back up, and attached this impromptu cape around my brother's neck. Without a moment's hesitation, he took a flying leap off the roof of the garage, a portly child, chin set with determination. It was impressive, until he landed right in the rose bushes. Scratched but undaunted, he climbed back onto the roof.

Jeannie chastised us both, insisting that superheroes only flew in movies with the help of strings, and that the real way to fly had been demonstrated by Mary Poppins. Since Jeannie was still living in Queens and her parents took her to R-rated movies, she had unquestionable authority over all matters of life, death, and flight. The three of us climbed back down in search of an umbrella. We climbed up again, having scored my father's big black umbrella, the kind that I would later recognize as being favored by funeral directors throughout the tri-state area. It took two of us to open the thing and hold it steady in the breeze. Jeannie instructed my brother in the proper stance: he was to hold the umbrella in his left hand and lift his right leg behind him, leaning into the wind. She was very convincing; a year or two later, she would persuade me that the swing in the neighborhood playground could actually circle around the bar. I was set for success until both chains broke simultaneously and I flew twenty feet through the air, without the benefit of cape or umbrella. But, for now, it was my brother who flew. He actually achieved some distance and cleared the rosebushes before ricocheting off a fence. That was the end of the experiments.

When I was in the throes of my Superman obsession during the mid-seventies, my brother was simply too young to fly along. And so I walked to the neighborhood store by myself in search of a Superman costume for Halloween.

Unfortunately, many other children had the same thought, and the store was completely sold out. Thankfully, they were out of the girls' costumes as well, so I wasn't forced into being a witch or a princess or an irony-free fairy. All that was left was Captain Marvel. The costume was bright red, with a yellow bolt of lightning down the front, emblazoned with the word "Shazam!" It was made of a tarp-like plastic, and to my six-year-old eyes it was beautiful. I bought it with my own money, seven dollars, which I paid with three two-dollar bills and a one. I was so proud. I brought the costume home, hiding it until a few minutes before I needed to leave for the school Halloween event, so no one could make me change my mind. My fear was that my mother would put me in a garbage bag with eyes and tell me I was a raisin. So I walked as casually as I could into the kitchen, wearing my Captain Marvel outfit with my hair slicked back. "I'm going to school now," I said, hoping to slip by without comment.

My fate was in the hands of my mother, my grand-mother, and my aunt, who were all sitting at the kitchen table, surrounded by a cloud of cigarette smoke and con-versation. "You can't go out like that," my mother exclaimed. Much to my dismay, they decided to help. All three ran down to the basement and started rummaging through the boxes. I loved my costume as it was, but they felt the need to accessorize, and they were unstoppable. I heard my mother's triumphant shout, my grandmother's laugh, and my aunt's hushed concern. My mother came up the stairs with her find. It was a wig. Not just any wig, but a giant afro. It was the kind of wig that Foxy Brown would pull a gun out of in *Coffee*, the blaxploitation classic. Unfortunately, Foxy's influence had not made it to suburban Long Island. I was cry-ing as my mother shoved the wig onto my slicked-back hair, completely oblivious to the cross-cultural travesty she was performing, never mind the impact on my budding experimentations with gender. Still, looking me up and down, she was dissatisfied. "You don't look like Captain Marvel because you don't feel like Captain Marvel. At least stand up straight." Little did I know that she was teaching me, very subtly, about self-confidence. I really could be whoever I wanted to be; I just had to believe it myself. Unfortunately, this version of Captain Marvel was not quite who I wanted to be. "You better keep that on," she warned. "We're going to drive by that school, and if you're not wearing it, you don't come home."

It was a crisp, sunny, fall day. The school tradition was that everyone came in costume. We would then process around the big playground in a strangely Celtic circular march, in which everyone could see everyone else. The other kids were more mainstream superheroes or cartoon characters or dinosaurs, and one kid looked like a bank robber behind his Jimmy Carter mask. The teachers saw me pass, and the expressions on their puzzled faces clearly said "Should we call her parents?" The play incident, however, was the only time that anyone called home; the entire neighborhood lived in fear of my grandfather, and the teachers were no exception. It was the girls in Care Bear costumes, oblivious to such adult subtleties, who beat me up.

I was not long for the playground, and the costume was not long for the world. It was completely flammable, an unfortunate fact that I discovered with a friend. We were Long Island kids: if you couldn't drink it, you burned it. At that point, I would do anything to stay under the radar.

Achashverosh: *The King Who Lets Everyone Else Run the Show. Well-Intentioned, He Makes the Mistakes Which Set the Whole Tragicomedy in Motion.*

By the time I was seven, my grandmother knew I was gay. Thanks to her, I discovered that I was far from the first in our family: one male relative was a hairdresser, one a renowned field hockey umpire, and another was literally "In the Navy." My Grandma gave me the gift of knowing, from an early age, that I never had a shot in hell at being straight. She told me to bide my time.

She was the only person I ever talked to when I was trying to decide between going to Barnard or going to Brandeis, knowing my boyfriend was on the fast track to marriage if I stayed home and went to Barnard. "You're worrying too much about his happiness," she told me. "He'll be fine. You should worry about your own happiness. Someone's gotta get out of here, and it's not going to be me." I looked at her, and saw that her hands were already shaking from the dementia that we both knew was coming. I remember thinking to myself that it felt like being handed a life jacket on a sinking ship.

When I was home on break, in my junior year at college, my grandmother, pride in her voice, called me from her upstairs apartment and told me to come up. She said she had a holiday surprise for me. She had seen a recipe on TV, and made it herself. The holiday was Purim. I was wary, but I figured: what was the worst it could be? Purim's main food groups are pastries and liquor.

The pastries, called hamantaschen, are triangle-shaped fruit- or poppy-seed-filled cookies meant to represent the hat, or the ears, of the holiday's villain, Haman. The booze was simply enough drink to get a person drunk. In fact, it is an edict of Jewish law to drink so much on Purim as not to know the difference between Mordechai, the hero of the Purim story, and his sworn enemy, Haman. I didn't watch PBS as religiously as my grandmother, but I was willing to bet that the station didn't have a feature on brewing one's own hooch. So I made an educated guess: hamantaschen.

When I walked into the apartment, I thought to myself: PBS got it right. These were not modernized bastardizations of an iconic Jewish food. These hamantaschen looked picture-perfect: three-cornered and golden brown, with poppy seeds glistening in the middle, and resting on doilies on my grandmother's best silver serving platter. They were a vision to behold. I almost started crying at this touching scene. This was far and away the sweetest thing anyone had ever done for me.

In reality, though, there were three major problems. First, my grandmother never baked. Second, I had a cold and couldn't smell a thing. Third, as I would soon discover, she had only watched half of the PBS Jewish Cooking special. The wrong half.

The perfect storm was heading my way. In life, one has a few culinary *Apocalypse Now* moments in which the only words one can whisper through the rising bile are "the horror, the horror." My first gefilte fish was one such moment. This was to be another.

"I had never heard of this holiday before," my grandmother confessed, "but I saw it on TV, and the cookies looked so pretty, and I'm so proud of you. I just had to make them!" Even the fact that she had watched a cooking program said a lot. My grandmother never watched cooking shows, on principle; she figured she didn't need them. The only culinary program she ever watched was Lidia Bastianach's Italian cooking show on PBS. The Italian American doyenne's cooking style reminded her of her own family's recipes. She took careful notes on each episode, but, to the best of anyone's knowledge, she never made any of the dishes she saw; rather, she enjoyed its validation of what she already did.

But now she had watched a cooking show featuring someone other than Lidia, she had baked, she had learned about a Jewish holiday, and she had done it all for me.

"The secret ingredient," she said, her excited eyes widening with pride as she saw me take one hamantaschen and open my mouth, "is love."

The pastry was right, but the filling had an oddly coarse texture, and a strangely greasy mouth feel. Beneath the perfect layer of poppy seeds, and encased in the perfect hamantaschen dough, was the distinct taste of *treyf*. She had said the secret ingredient was love, but I realized that it was pork.

For a brief moment, my grandmother turned around and I took the opportunity to spit the hamantaschen out and jammed it in my pocket. Loose Italian sausage meat. In a cookie. With poppy seeds. It was fusion cooking gone terribly wrong, and it wouldn't be appearing in a Joan Nathan Jewish cookbook anytime soon. In the meantime, there was not enough mouthwash in the world to rid me of the awful taste and the sinking feeling that I had just shot years of good eating habits to hell.

My aversion to pork predated my attraction to Judaism. In high school, we had to dissect fetal pigs, and so the smells of pork and formaldehyde became completely linked in my mind. Add to that a newly scrupulous observance of kashrut and vegetarianism, and the taste of pork was enough to make me want to die.

I had to know for sure. "Grandma, what's in that?" "It's hamantaschen. I did exactly what the recipe said." "So what did the recipe say?" "Well, I'm not really sure, because I missed the first half. But I know that it was a cookie, with poppy seeds on top, and that the name was *ham-in-taschen*." She enunciated each syllable as if it were a separate word. Ham. In. Taschen.

This is exactly where my brain imploded.

"You mean you put ham in the taschen?" "No, we don't cook with ham, sweetie. It's Italian sausage, only done more like a pig-in-a-blanket." "Oh, so you mean pork sausage?" "Well, I heard the name was ham-in-taschen, and I knew it was a holiday of turning things upside down." Ham-in-taschen. The ham part was bad enough. But "taschen" gave it an extra level of meaning. Leafing through a book on a lecherous professor's coffee table that semester, I had discovered that Taschen was a publisher whose catalog included many sexually explicit "art" books. Pig-in-a-blanket, indeed.

My grandmother had determined that Purim was a funny holiday where everything you thought about Judaism was turned on its ear. Why shouldn't the hamantaschen, the ears of the villain, be filled with ham? Clever woman that she was, my grandmother had seen the finished product on television for a brief moment, learned its complicated name, taken what information she could about the holiday, and worked backward to make the recipe from scratch—all for the sake of reaching out to me and to the person I had become. She could have just bought the hamantaschen from the store.

As my eyes watered from a tripped gag reflex, my grandmother thought that I was overwhelmed at her beautiful gesture. She was half right, and I was not about to correct her. "There's no need to cry," she said. "I love you. This is what family does."

8

Passover

I'll Be Home for Pesach

In the first month, on the fourteenth day of the
month, at twilight, there shall be a Passover offering
to the Eternal, and on the fifteenth day of that month
the Eternal's Feast of Unleavened Bread. You shall
eat unleavened bread for seven days.

—Leviticus 23:5–6

Why Is This Phone Call Different?

In the days before Caller ID, I relied solely on the
hairs on my neck to tell me that my mother was calling. Half-
mast meant a reasonable chance at a ten-minute nontoxic
conversation. On this particular day, my hair stood at full
attention as the telephone's ring elicited its Pavlovian
response.

"We're making arrangements," she stated. Arrangements. My mind reeled at this choice of words.

"Arrangements" conjured images of random family
funerals. I envisioned open caskets with slut-red lipstick
applied to the otherwise chaste elderly deceased, prompting
distant relatives to say, "She looks so lovely, doesn't she?"

My mother didn't even make "arrangements" when
pets died. After seven to twelve years of dutiful service, a
beloved furry companion's remains always received the
same final disposition. It was quickly mummified in one of

her "good" towels. Egyptian cotton was frequently chosen, both for its religious symbolism and for its high thread count.

For Lucky, our morbidly obese housecat, death came quietly as she sprawled in the morning sunlight. In life, Lucky had looked like a toothless miniature Holstein cow. In death, she looked much the same. Despite the chill of death, the sun had kept her warm all day. This, in turn, kept us from noticing her demise. By the time my mother came home from work and noticed the dead cat on her bed, rigor mortis had set in. She lifted the body, and it looked like a furry manhole cover, limbs akimbo. This called for a larger towel. No expense was spared as my mother wrapped the oblate body in her jacquard holiday finest and then slipped it into a garbage pail a few doors down the block.

What "arrangements," then, could my mother possibly have in store for me?

"The spring holidays are coming, and we want to make plans to fly you home."

I breathed a sigh of relief that neither I, nor anyone else I knew, was being interred. "Spring holidays" was a surprisingly sensitive interfaith phrase. My mother knew that her almost Jewish daughter was not going to come home from Jerusalem for Easter.

The Questionable Child

I had always had fond memories of Easter. Others in my family relished the delights of Easter lamb and ham, but, as a little girl, I preferred the chocolate bunnies, in a very specific way. Each year, on the night before Easter, I crept into the dining room where the chocolate bunnies were stacked. Pyramids of leporine confections, still in their boxes, beckoned. I stealthily approached my quarry. Using a thumbnail that I had grown and sharpened for the occasion, I ritually removed the hard candy eyes of each bunny and tucked them into the pocket of my little terry robe. Then, I returned the blinded bunnies to their boxes and neatly restacked them. Except for the missing eyes, they looked entirely untouched. I tiptoed back to my room and piled the candy eyes on the bed in front of me. I devoured them and went to sleep: an angelic blonde, blue-eyed child with visions of candy eyeballs dancing through her head.

The next morning, I would awaken to the sound of screams. The first year, the screams were followed by my mother's indignant declaration "I'm taking these back to the store!" The second year, it was "Which one of you psychos got into the bunnies?" By the third year, they had found out. It must have been the chocolate stains on my bathrobe that gave me away. The screams were replaced by the hushed acknowledgment "Look, she did it again." Perhaps it was the fear of having raised a child capable of making chocolate Easter bunnies look as though they had just seen the contents of the Ark of the Covenant, but my parents never confronted me. And now they wanted me home for the spring holidays. Maybe they knew that, this time, the bunnies were safe.

Affliction Is Relative

If I went home, not only would the chocolate be off-limits: so would everything else. Passover with my parents and no kosher kitchen would mean a punishing week on the Macaroon Diet. The kosher-for-Passover coconut macaroons my family bought on sale every year for my Jewish uncle smelled like cheap suntan lotion, and stiffened into charcoal briquettes when exposed to air. Like the towering Italian panettone, or the traditional door-stop of a fruitcake, the Passover macaroon was for display purposes only. Besides, the constipation would have killed me.

For me, one of the newly discovered joys of Passover was keeping a kosher home. Having cleaned dozens of houses all over Israel to make ends meet, I had an intimate knowledge of the traditional laws of kashrut, as well as of many a prominent Israeli's underwear drawer. We are a kinky people.

"I'd really prefer not to come home right now. I'll be seeing you all in a few months, anyway," I said. This was not the right answer. My mother proceeded to give me all the reasons why I had to come home. Backed into a corner, I had no choice but to deliver the death blow: "Ma, the kitchen isn't kosher. You can't cook for me." The worst thing you can tell a Sicilian mother is that she can't cook for you. This was like stabbing her in the heart, and it killed me to have to say it. At least when my eighty-year-old grandmother was told not to cook anymore, there was real and present danger afoot. We were afraid of being immolated by the olive-oil-driven fires that would flare up every time she fried an egg. The cigarette perpetually dangling from her lips certainly couldn't have helped. At least twice a week, the fire alarm went off in her kitchen on the top floor of our two-family home. Grandma's burgeoning dementia and defective hearing aid left her blissfully unaware of the threat, to herself and to everyone else in the house. My grandparents had moved out to Long Island with us from Brooklyn after my grandmother was mugged at knifepoint for a box of cookies. Now, in the years after my grandfather's death, my grandmother lived upstairs alone. It felt like only a matter of time before our home would be reduced to cinders. I imagined identifying the culprit to the authorities as if I were solving a game of Clue: "I suggest Grandma Bellafiore, in the kitchen, with a pack of Salem Lights."

My mother, however, was in the prime of her cooking years. There was a long pause, during which my mother processed the information that she could not cook for me.

From her perspective, this meant she was no longer useful in this world. I took this moment of silence to consolidate my mixed feelings about a Passover visit. I felt torn between two worlds, one with binding rules that demanded stringent observance, and the other Jewish.

Our verbal sparring continued. And then she asked me, "What do I do in this situation?" I said, "Mom, the problem is that the kitchen isn't kosher, and there's really nothing that you can do about it." We had another long pause and she said, "I'll take care of it." "You can't take care of this, Ma." "I'll take care of it." "Mom, you *can't* take care of it." "*I'll take care of it.*" Click.

When my mother says she'll "take care of it," you know that the conversation has ended. If it was possible, the hairs on my neck were standing up even higher than before the phone first rang.

I had reason to be nervous. My mother's only previous Jewish ritual experience was a bust. Her first seder took place at the home of the senior physician from the practice where she worked. The house was grand. It was beautiful. It was gated. And the glint of sliver was everywhere on that table. One of the centerpieces was a beautiful silver three-tiered matzah tray. On each level was a hand-rolled shmurah matzah. Shmurah matzah is specially supervised from the moment the grain is harvested to prevent any possible contact with water. It is usually misshapen, slightly burnt, and instantly desiccating. If regular matzah is akin to standard issue New York–style pizza, then shmurah matzah is its super-thin, crispy, and charred New Haven cousin. At $25 a box, shmurah matzah is a far cry from the bread of affliction.

In this case, the physician's family did not guard the shmurah matzah enough. My mother was seated next to the matzah tray. No one had told her how long the first part of the seder was going to be. She was getting very hungry, and the parsley wasn't cutting it. So she started sneaking off pieces of matzah tiny enough to be eaten quietly. Not content to eat just one, she nibbled on all three. When the time came in the seder to display the matzah, only blackened crumbs remained. The group was stunned. Rather than be embarrassed, my mother thought this was hysterical.

Passover aside, my mother was familiar with dietary restrictions. When I was in high school, I loved listening to the Smiths. I treasured their album *Meat Is Murder* and was bereft when my tape disappeared. Within a week, it was discovered in the glove compartment of my mother's car, and, within a month later, my mother became vegan. The rest of us, who remained omnivorous, marveled at her ability to cook anything alive or dead despite this radical shift. She would still cook spiral ham and filet mignon and twelve kinds of fish for Christmas Eve. When asked about her decision, she would only look her questioner straight in the eye and say, "If you choose to eat dead bodies, that's your business." My mother had all of the righteous indignation of Jules from *Pulp Fiction*. Perhaps I should have left the collected works of Mahatma Gandhi around, instead.

I could not understand at the time, but my mother was changing faster than any of us. She just hid it better. After I converted to Judaism, her private research on kashrut led her to keep one pot aside reserved just for her pasta. There were no theological or philosophical explanations offered, only the one-time utterance: "Touch that pot and I'll kill you."

We had all assumed that my mother was still scarred from an incident years earlier. A school project about world landmarks went terribly wrong when my father and I tried to create a plaster version of the Roman Coliseum. We used my mother's best stew pot, but forgot to grease the sides. The resulting cement block had to be removed with hammer and chisel, forever scarring the pot—as well as my mother's confidence in both my academic future and my father's judgment.

This confidence had already been severely diminished by two other incidents. First, there was the time my mother went into the hospital for a hysterectomy and left us in my father's care. He did not know how to cook and was too embarrassed to tell anyone; also, my mother had a policy against having any outside help. He ordered Chinese food for himself, which my brother and I did not like. We were left eating the only thing he knew how to make, Black Forest cake. The illicit pleasure of having cake three times a day wore off remarkably fast.

The second incident took place one Easter morning when, ever the ersatz scientist, my father lit a match under a small bottle filled with gasoline and topped with a vinegar-soaked egg. He had expected the small implosion to create a vacuum and suck the softened egg into the bottle. To everyone but my grandfather's surprise, the bottle shattered, and my mother's new curtains instantly caught on fire. Their high polyester content ensured maximum pageantry and emotional carnage.

In a family where Easter led to four-alarm fires, the four questions of Passover seemed tame.

Opening the Door

"Come into my office and use my phone right now," the director of the yeshiva said, rushing into my classroom, "There is an emergency in America."

I could barely keep up with him as we rushed to his office. My hands were shaking so much that I twice misdialed the phone. The director's eyes were fixed on me, and I could tell that he was already searching for meaningful things to say about my loss. I was sure that my grandmother had burned the house down. My knuckles were white, as I clutched the director's large chair.

As soon as my mother heard my voice, she began to laugh. I was less amused; my mother's cackle can be heard across rooms, and the director's expression was changing from sympathetic to confused. Still, I was relieved, because her laughter meant that everyone was still alive, and that no property had been irreparably damaged. Finally, she took a breath, and began to speak: "I have a story for you."

"I'll take care of it," she had insisted. And she certainly had taken care of it, in her own very clever way. My mother may not be Jewish, but she is resourceful and well read enough to recall the advertisement on the front page of the *New York Times* every Friday that said, "Jewish girls: Light your Shabbat candles!" So she called Brooklyn, home to Chabad Lubavitch, a group of Chasidic Jews who take upon themselves the mission of bringing other Jews closer to God. My mother called Chabad to come make the house kosher for Passover—in particular, to take care of the oven. Now, going to the Lubavitch to take care of an oven is like killing a fly with a tank. The fly will die, but there will be serious collateral damage.

"I told the nice lady on the phone that we needed a kosher kitchen for my daughter for Passover." Those words were matzah from heaven to the woman on the other end of the line. The woman from Chabad was thrilled to hear that there was a girl studying in yeshiva in Jerusalem who wanted to come home for Passover, and couldn't unless she could keep kosher. It must have been moving to her that this girl's mother wanted nothing more than to have her home and to accommodate her with the food that she needed. "Other mothers wouldn't care, but I want to go the extra distance," my mother had said. Competitive parenting was an Olympic sport, and she was going for the gold.

This spiraled into an urgent matter for all involved. The woman assured my mother that the full force of Chabad would be brought to bear upon her kitchen. My mother, for her part, thought this woman was just delightful. "She made everything so easy!" she marveled. She recalled the conversation with much love and respect for her newfound compatriot across the cultural divide. This from a woman whose first words to me upon hearing of my plans to convert to Judaism were, "Does this mean you are going to move to Brooklyn, wear a wig, and have twelve kids?" Now, she was inviting Brooklyn into her home. An appointment was made for the very next day.

A note was left for my grandmother, as she was the only one who would be home. It read, "Someone is coming to take care of the oven." It could have been someone to read the gas meter, it could have been an appliance technician; frankly, it could have been anyone except the person who actually showed up.

The doorbell rang and my grandmother made her way down the steps, opened the door, and passed out. The last thing she saw before fainting was a six-foot-two Chasidic man with a big black beard, sunglasses, and a blow torch. As she was passing out, she swore, "*Merda, merda, angelo della morte* ("Oh shit, oh shit, the Angel of Death!") She thought it was her time. Later she confessed to me that she was most disturbed by the fact that the Angel of Death was a Jew.

In the meantime, this poor man, who had no doubt come to our home with only the best of intentions, was met with a small, traumatized Sicilian woman passed out on the floor. Rather than run away, he kindly waited for my woozy grandmother to recover sufficiently for a glass of water—and some literature. He also checked the oven. On top of the pamphlets he left a note that said, "Self-cleaning oven. Kashering not necessary."

9

Lag B'Omer

The Work of the Chariot

But they who trust in the Eternal shall renew their strength as eagles grow new plumes: They shall run and not grow weary; they shall march and not grow faint.
                                                    —Isaiah 40:31

The thirty-third day of the Omer is a respite from a period of mourning that spans seven weeks, from Passover to Shavuot. Some sages have said that, on Lag B'Omer, a scourge on Rabbi Akiva's students was lifted. Deep spiritual meaning is also attached to this minor holiday because of its association with one of the greatest students of Rabbi Akiva, the mystic Rabbi Shimon Bar Yochai. In Israel, the holiday is celebrated by huge bonfires and outdoor games, and is a special favorite of teenagers.

I am not especially mystical, and I have a healthy respect for fire. On our honeymoon, Lisa and I stayed in a country house in the Poconos lent to us by friends. Joan and her husband were kind enough to leave a bottle of Veuve Clicquot in the fridge, and candlesticks on the table. When it came time for Shabbat, we put candles in the candlesticks and lit them, somehow ignoring the fact that the candlesticks were themselves made of wood. Suffice it to say that the evening ended dramatically but not romantically, as we rushed to put out the flames.

Despite our misadventure, the connection between youth and fire is universal, as is the search for enlightenment. And so, on this numinous day, I sometimes recall one of the earliest rabbinic mystical themes, known as Ma'aseh Merkavah, "the work of the chariot." Merkavah literature is based on the story of Ezekiel's ascending chariot. It is reserved for only the most knowledgeable and brilliant minds. Jewish tradition teaches that whoever engages with these activities must be wise, well prepared, and at least forty years old. The characters in the short play below met none of those qualifications, and yet they experienced a unique ascent into an ecstatic realm all their own. Like the kabbalists of old, they had only their creativity to propel them to greater heights.

Narrator: Lazy summer day circa 1983. August. Garbage day. The stifling heat and the stink make the blacktop shimmer. Summer camps and other supervised activities ended weeks ago, and suburban children are left to their own devices. Two girls around twelve years old are standing at the end of a long driveway. Of late, their afternoons are spent pulling each other around in a plastic milk crate with a long rope. No wheels are ever attached. The plastic edges of the crate melt as they scrape the blacktop. Sparks become visible once critical speed is achieved.

Now they are looking for a new milk crate in the garbage pile, having destroyed the last one, Sparky II, the day before.

(Cue the music: the Vangelis theme to *Chariots of Fire*)

Jeannie: It sucks that we have to go back to school in a week.

Andrea: Yeah.

Jeannie: We should do something special before it's over. Like, really big. We should totally do something from history.

Andrea: Yeah.

Narrator: Somewhere in the pile, a large red milk crate in good shape is found. Jackpot. It is examined for quite some time. The girls puzzle over the crate silently, with all of the gravitas of experts at a pre-launch inspection of the space shuttle. Consensus is reached, and the girls nod in approval.

Jeannie: It needs something.

Andrea: Yeah. But what? It's already red and you used up all my stickers.

(Long pause.)

Jeannie (deadpan)*:* Fire.

Andrea: Fire? Damn it, Jeannie, you're crazy. Fire is your answer to everything lately. Ever since that school burned down on *Little House*, that's all you think about. We're totally going to get in trouble. And, like, I know way more than I should about field-dressing an injury. Pretty soon someone's going to get hurt and need more than just Popsicle sticks and Band-aids, and then my mother's going to kill us all.

Jeannie (Indignantly, but with majestic poise as the music swells)*:* Yes. You are right. We might get hurt. We *will* get hurt. So we should make it good. Just imagine this crate being pulled down the driveway *on fire!* It will be awesome! Like in the movies. Anyway, wasn't there a movie called *Chariots of Fire*? What was that about?

Andrea: I don't know. Something about people running in slow motion. Wow, you know, maybe you're right. Maybe they were running away from fire. But slow.

Jeannie: You should ask your grandfather. He knows everything.

Andrea: Agreed.

Jeannie: And anyways, it would totally be your father's fault, 'cause he keeps extra fireworks in the garage in the first place.

Andrea: Agreed.

Jeannie: We should probably use your brother to pull us. He runs pretty fast, and he won't be expecting the roman candles.

Andrea: Oh my God! He *so* won't see that coming!

Jeannie: Wait, didn't they also have chariots in Rome? Maybe that movie was about Rome.

Andrea: Totally! You are so smart. This will be great.

Jeannie: Okay, so I'll get your brother to pull us, and you'll ask your grandfather what a chariot of fire is.

Andrea: Agreed. This will be the best end-of-summer *ever*.

The ending is shrouded in mystery. The reader is free to imagine skin abrasions, a patchy burned lawn, and damaged pride. Decades later, Jeannie and I are professionals, with families of our own. She is an educator and I am a rabbi, both of us in positions where we teach and take care of others. Even though we would never endorse such behavior, despite having initiated it ourselves, from time to time at family gatherings we look at one another with a knowing smile. We are reminded of a time when the flight of body and soul was possible, sparks flew with youthful abandon, and the sky was close enough to touch.

10

Shavuot

Take
Two Tablets

How do we accept a convert? . . . We say to him, "Why
do you wish to convert? Don't you know that Israel
in these times are suffering, oppressed, downtrodden,
and troubles afflict them?" If he responds, "Yes, I
know, and I am not worthy in sharing in that burden,"
we accept him immediately.

—Maimonides, Mishneh Torah,
Issurei Biah 14:1

I am so not worthy.   —Andrea, in the *mikvah*

Learning under the Influence

His blue eyes twinkled. When he looked at you, he
could tell immediately if you had been bad or good. He
reminded me of Santa. Not just any Santa, but the one from
Miracle on 34th Street, which talks about Santa being like
an angel. Years later, I would learn that, in Judaism, an
angel, *malach*, is not a flighty being with a halo. Rather, an
angel is God's messenger, and that is precisely who I had just
met.

It was my first encounter with Rabbi Al Axelrad, the
Brandeis Hillel rabbi. He was walking around the campus
introducing himself, the first week of classes. I had never met
a rabbi before, but clearly many people had met him. He was
surrounded by groupies, people who seemed to know him and

genuinely like him. I quickly learned that he was not a proselytizer but had a clear agenda: to make the world a peaceful place. Rabbi Al was the most aggressive pacifist I have ever met. He had causes about which he was passionate, but, most of all, he was passionate about connecting with students and helping them on their paths. When I met him, I knew very little about Judaism, but I did understand that here was an extraordinary member of the clergy, rooted in his traditions yet in touch with the world in all its diversity.

When Rabbi Al celebrated twenty-five years at Brandeis, a tribute book was compiled, with the title *A Gentle Giant*. On the back is a quotation that epitomizes his work: "The Torah is not written down in any book. It flows from one soul to another." For generations of students, Rabbi Al has been someone from whom Torah flows.

A year after we met, our paths crossed again. This time, I made an appointment with him, walked into his office, and said, "I want to be Jewish." He smiled his great big smile and replied, "I'm going to know you for the rest of your life."

There is a tradition in Judaism of turning a potential convert away three times before accepting the person as a student. Rabbi Al did not do that. Instead, when he heard my story, he told me, "Your life has made it complicated enough for you to get here. I don't need to discourage you." And so we began our studies. What was most important to him was that my knowledge of Judaism be experiential and not solely academic. And, in fact, as a pre-med student, I could fit no Jewish studies courses into my schedule, so I had to do my learning in other ways. The only class I took in the Department of Near Eastern and Judaic Studies was a survey course on Islam.

I started going to Shabbat services throughout the Boston area. At first, I liked the long-distance relationship model of theology, keeping religion to something I did once a week in a different town. Even though I was at a Jewish-sponsored university and my attendance at services would have been welcomed, I was still embarrassed by how different I was from many of the other students. No one from my high school had ever attended Brandeis, and no one from Brandeis came from anywhere like my high school. In my public school, I had excelled, but I was still woefully unprepared for college. My cultural references were different, and socioeconomically I was in a different class. I started off at Brandeis not knowing anyone, and, when I made friends, it was mostly with people who were not Jewish.

As I became more involved with Judaism, I made the surprising and unpleasant discovery that not only were most of my friends not Jewish, but some were anti-Semitic as well. My politics were nascent in every sense, and I was unprepared for being accused of what one woman called "over-identifying with the Zionist aggressor." This seemed hypocritical, coming from a woman who was so belligerent that she used casual conversation as an opportunity to pummel her opponent with rhetoric. At the time, I had a witty comeback, but I was embarrassed at how ignorant I felt. I used this thrashing as an impetus to learn more about the politics of developing a Jewish identity.

It is not surprising, then, that I spent the beginning of my Jewish journey by segregating my Jewish experiences from the rest of my life. This was akin to exploring one's sexuality far from home. You could test the waters but still feel safe. However, I soon reached a point where I needed to integrate my life.

It took a lot for me to come out as a Jew on campus. Going to my first Shabbat service at Brandeis was a huge step. I walked in and saw someone from my class leading the service, playing guitar with his eyes closed, and using the Reform prayer book. I loved it. The experience was peaceful and uplifting, almost to the point of being a spiritual cliché. I am not someone who sings, yet I found myself singing songs I had never heard. I had been to enough services, by that point, to realize how special this was.

As I advanced in my studies, practical questions of conversion came up during my conversations with Rabbi Al. He suggested a conversion in Boston, under Conservative auspices, in keeping with my level of observance: I had started keeping kosher and living a fairly traditional Jewish life. The only thing I had not yet done was to change to a kosher meal plan. I could just imagine my parents opening the Brandeis bill and seeing an additional itemization for kosher food. My decision to change religion would be hard enough for them; given the importance of food in my family, changing my eating habits—and their needing to pay for this—would be entirely too much for them to handle.

The prospect of becoming Jewish became more and more compelling. One of the other students at Hillel, Sam, had been raised with a strong Jewish upbringing in Pittsburgh. He had pointed me toward a book that proved formative, Mordecai Kaplan's *Judaism as a Civilization*. Growing up in suburban America, surrounded by—and part of—the Christian majority, it had been hard for me to imagine what it would be like to choose, and live, a Jewish life. For the first time, I was able to envision Judaism as an American ideal in its own right, a religion that not only was viable in the Diaspora but thrived alongside other religions. While Sam and I were working together on a project for Hillel, one of the other students looked at us and said, "So where are you guys going to go to rabbinical school?" For Sam, the question made sense: he was already on-track to apply. All I could say was, "I'm not even Jewish, how could I ever become a rabbi?" We all laughed, but it stuck in my head.

I thought about my life, and all the reasons I wanted to become a doctor. My mother was a brilliant medical billing director, and no doctor she worked for would say no to a request to employ her daughter. Thanks to this blatant nepotism, I had been interfacing with patients since I was fourteen years old. And thanks to lax employee guidelines, my work had been substantial; I was drawing blood before I knew how to drive. My real goal, though, was to work with people with HIV and contribute on the medical end of that fight, to give compassionate care to people who were suffering. But as time passed, I realized a few things. First: everyone I wanted to treat was going to die. I was an ACT-UP campus activist, and I had no illusions about the message that came from the Bush administration, that AIDS was far from a priority. Second: no matter how hard I worked, I was not nearly good enough in science to be helpful. Any sense of ability and accomplishment that I had from high school science had been erased by my poor academic performance at Brandeis. Third: I wanted to walk with people in a different part of the life cycle, not only at the end of their lives. Fourth: I still wanted to help people, but the language that was most compelling to me was Judaism, not medicine.

Becoming Jewish, and then a rabbi, had been described to me as almost impossible. The "almost" gave me hope. If there was a one-in-a-million chance that I could do this, even if it would take me my whole life, I was going to. I would do it to the detriment of everything else, whether that meant abandoning career plans I had held for twenty years, the wishes of my family, or the feelings of friends who did not like converts or gays or Jews. I could not become the person I felt I needed to be in a way that would please anybody else, so I decided to do it my own way. At the same time, my increased involvement in the Jewish community was leading to an increased awareness of its internal politics, and I learned about the issues surrounding conversion and Jewish status, particularly the fact that the nature of one's conversion determines the identity of one's children. As a woman, I was especially aware of traditional Judaism's belief in matrilineal descent, according to which a mother's religious identity determines that of her child. I needed to convert in a way that was right for me and, above all, for those who would come after me. Whatever else Judaism meant, I knew it involved more than my single self. So I went back to Rabbi Al and asked, "How do I do this in such a way that there will be no question about my children's status?" He insisted that nothing I could do would make everyone happy, but that if I wanted to reach the highest common denominator, I would need to live in Israel and convert under Orthodox auspices; he made clear that this would be very hard. I responded, "Sign me up."

I had never imagined that pursuing my life goals would necessitate going to the Middle East. I had already planned out my life: I was going to go to college, go to medical school, work, cure AIDS, and die. I had meager spiritual aspirations and few personal dreams. But I did miss God. As a child, on some level I frequently felt in the presence of something larger than myself; someone was watching over me, and I sensed that it was more than my grandfather with his BB gun at the window, or my mother looking through my dresser. In more recent years, I had been hard hit by a series of losses. My grandfather had died of lung cancer and my cousin had died of AIDS. I had dealt with rejection when I came out as gay. I knew my life was set up to be tough. I had left the Catholic Church, saddened by my experiences there, and I had come to Brandeis and felt invisible and scared, academically and socially overwhelmed. Yet I knew that, in some way, I was washing up onto the shores of the next chapter of my life.

I look back at this time and associate it with *Rosh Chodesh*, the beginning of each Jewish month. The night sky is dark, and the moon cannot yet be seen. Even in the darkness, we come together to celebrate, knowing that the moon will wax larger until it is full, and trusting that the darkness will recede. As the Talmud teaches, "All beginnings are hard."

The Wandering Jew-by-Choice

So how does one join this people? We learn from looking at the story of Abraham, the first Jew. The way the story usually is told, God appears to Abraham out of nowhere and tells him to go to the Land of Canaan, "the land that I will show you." Abraham then totally reorients his life and sets off for this new locale. His GPS is his faith in God. However, if you look a few verses earlier in the Torah, you will see that Abraham already knew that he was going to Canaan, and in fact he had already begun his journey there. So why did he need God to direct him?

One possibility is that Abraham has been paralyzed by grief. In a very short time span, his father and one of his brothers have died. Another brother does not accompany him, his nephew Lot is a low-life, and his wife Sarah is barren. He is not getting any younger. Everything he has imagined for his life and everything he has taken for granted in terms of his life's direction is now different. In this situation, God does not set him on a new path, but gently reminds him of where he had been going before tragedy struck. Abraham needed direction, and God helped him find it—but Abraham was already on the way. A major part of becoming Jewish involves seeing how this path is a continuation of a journey already begun.

God blessed Abraham by saying he would become greater than he was; his descendants would be like the sand of the sea and the stars of the sky. Another way of seeing this is to say that God wants us to be who we are, only more so. Some people think that the God of the Torah has a chip on the shoulder, but this couldn't be further from the truth. My experience has been that God wants us to succeed, that God has a sense of humor, and that God encourages us to be tenacious in finding our paths. This is why, I believe, Jewish tradition teaches that a potential convert should be turned away three times: not to discourage us, but to tell us that we need to be tough. To become a member of a people that has been persecuted, one has to be willing to be an advocate and an ambassador, not just for oneself but also for others. The meek may inherit the earth, but to become a Jew requires other qualities.

And so I persisted. I did what Rabbi Al said, and made plans to study in Israel after graduation. He told me about a magical place called Pardes, where Jews of various denominations could come and study. As a Protestant, I had been very aware of internal religious divisions, especially given my parents' experience of ostracism in their Catholic–Protestant union. At Brandeis, I had seen similar divisiveness among Jewish denominations. I loved the thought of learning in a place where people came together instead. More than anything, I wanted to learn everything from everyone, and Pardes seemed the best place to go.

I flew to Tel Aviv on Delta, on a flight full of singing missionaries from Kansas. The woman sitting next to me spent the length of the flight telling me all about the goodness of Jesus, and the evils of gays and abortion. She seemed very excited, and assumed everyone around her felt the same way. I focused my energies on reading and rereading the emergency information card. Realizing that I had another seven hours left on the flight, I took a quantity of Benadryl sufficient to fell a bull elephant, and slept for the rest of the flight. When the plane landed, I made my way to the exit. The door opened, and I walked down the steps to the tarmac. It was late summer. The light was incredibly bright and the sky was bluer than blue, unlike anything I had seen. The heat was also intense, and I was wearing four layers of clothing, having worn everything that I did not have room to pack.

I had to close my eyes for a few seconds to adjust to the light, and when I opened them I noticed many groups of soldiers holding guns. They were looking suspiciously at everyone who got off the plane, particularly the rowdy missionary group. It took two hours to reclaim my ransacked luggage, and then I had to get my student visa. "Why are you here?" the young solider asked. "To study in yeshiva," I replied. "What's your mother's Hebrew name?" "She's not Jewish." "So you're not Jewish. Why are you studying in yeshiva? Are you with these people?" At this, the soldier gestured toward the missionaries with her gun. "No," I said quickly, "I'm trying to get *away* from these people. That's the point of this trip." She smiled, stamped my visa, and I was in. Coming back from Israel years later, I was on a flight full of Orthodox Jews. Going through customs back in New York, the agent saw my modern American garb and said to me, "You should stay away from those people," referring to the sea of Jews around me. "I am one of those people," I replied.

Once I escaped the missionaries and Ben Gurion Airport, I had to find my way to Jerusalem. I got on the right bus, but it was going ninety miles per hour and I could not read the signs quickly enough to get off at the right stop. The bus sped through Jerusalem and on toward the south. I did not manage to disembark until Be'er Sheva, far to the south in the Negev. I looked around and saw that everything was flat and dry and not at all as I had imagined Jerusalem. I fought my way back onto a bus headed back north, and this time got off at Jerusalem's Central Bus Station. In a small country, I had managed to be on a bus for at least twelve traumatizing hours. I made my way to a hostel in the middle of town. A few days later, I visited Pardes and found an apartment. And so the City of David became my city as well.

One of my new neighbors, Rhea, was from England. She introduced herself to me as soon as I moved in. Soon we were having tea every afternoon and talking. She had trouble getting around, and I helped her by going to the cor-

ner store and doing her shopping. We bonded over the skanky
cats who infested the neighborhood, as they did most neighborhoods in Jerusalem. We shared our food and conversation
with them. Rhea was incredibly proud of having made a *kippah* for President Clinton, which he wore when he visited
Yad Vashem. It was black, with a trademark dove. She made
me one, exactly the same. When Lisa went to study in Israel,
during the early months of our relationship, she too met Rhea,
and, not knowing my connection with her, asked her to
make me a kippah. This one was a rainbow kippah, also
with that trademark dove. The first time I saw it, the co-
incidence took my breath away. The kippah brought back a
flood of memories of the kindness Rhea had shown me in
those first months in Jerusalem.

Although I did not know it at the time, the dove would
have great significance in my Jewish life. Later during my first
year in Jerusalem, I was sitting with friends at their Shabbat table, singing Shabbat songs. One had the refrain "*Yonah
matzah bo manoach*—on that day, the dove found rest." The
allusion was to the dove that left Noah's ark, finding a resting place on the olive tree on Shabbat. I loved the image, as
Shabbat had become so central to my Jewish life. I also
liked how *Yonah* could be translated as either "dove" or
"pigeon." As in English, the birds were related. This reminded
me of my Uncle Dominic's pigeon-raising days. I loved how
it referred to the prophet Jonah, because of the many times
that I had felt myself in the belly of the whale. And finally,
I liked how, in modern Israel, Yonah was a name that was
gender-neutral. Knowing that when Jews are called up to the
Torah, they are called up with their parents' names, I thought
this name might make it easier for any child of mine to move
with ease throughout the Jewish world. When it came time
to choose a Hebrew name, Yonah was the name I chose.

All this time, I was learning. Soon after my arrival at
Pardes, I sat down and read the English translation of the

Talmud from beginning to end. What I loved the most was that it read like the *Farmer's Almanac*, which had fascinated me as a child. It took me back to my younger self's inquisitiveness about the nature of the world.

My mother had subscribed to the *Star*, the *National Enquirer*, and the *Globe*, and my father would read the *New York Times*, folded that special way for his commute on the Long Island Rail Road, a folding I thought of as "executive origami." But the *Farmer's Almanac* was the only reading material that had interested me in my house. Here was my exposure to the agricultural world, complete with crazy psychics, and agricultural laws promising either bounty or death. I loved the wood engravings at the top of each almanac section, and how each day had its own description. Each annual edition was like its own encyclopedia. It fed my curiosity about how the world worked, about what was going on in history, art, or the night sky. When I discovered the Talmud, I approached it in the same way, searching for wisdom with the comfort of knowing that people had done everything before, and that any answer could be found if one knew where to look. "December 18th: Wind rolled snow into balls, Howe, Indiana. . . . January 30th: Raccoons mate now."

My Jewish learning, that first year in Jerusalem, was especially reminiscent of the *Almanac*'s agricultural focus, because Israelis were preparing for a *shemitta* year. The shemitta year is the sabbatical, the seventh year, on which the land rests and no farming is allowed. One of my teachers was an expert on shemitta. His sprightliness belied his age, thick glasses, and long beard; when we took hikes, he was like a gazelle, leaving everyone else behind.

Another teacher taught me how to chant Torah. The first section of Torah I learned dealt with the red heifer, whose ashes are used to purify people who have come into contact with death. I became interested in studying texts about the desert Tabernacle and the First and Second Temples, where the purification ceremony and other rituals occurred. I was struck by how the Ark of the Covenant was a quintessentially Jewish object yet was commonly depicted in a way that felt very familiar. When I was a child, I had an interest in ancient Egyptian culture. In the years when there were traveling Tutankhamen exhibitions, this interest was far from rare, but with me it bordered on the obsessive. I knew all about the canopic jars that the Egyptians used for storing embalmed viscera, a part of the process of mummification. While other kids bought comic books, I saved my allowance for Wallace Budge's book on hieroglyphs and his edition of *The Book of the Dead*. I believe that the silence of the Torah around death and the afterlife, and its insistence on choosing life, is a rejection of this Egyptian legacy. It was fascinating to think about which aspects of Judaism included the Egyptian culture that had surrounded the Israelites for so long, and which were intended to reject them.

A byproduct of these discoveries was that my studies gave me something new to talk about with my father; he is a multigenerational Freemason with membership in a number of different Masonic orders, some of which share a deep knowledge of the architecture of the Temple. On my childhood trips to Pennsylvania, we had sometimes made an excursion to a model Tabernacle, built to scale by the Mennonites. However impressive it was, the model seemed lonely. It just wasn't right without real people—and now I had the knowledge to imagine them as part of the story. Ultimately, the Tabernacle and the Temple were not about architecture; they were about the relationship between humans and the divine. Not only did the sacrificial system seem to me a great way to make sure people were fed, and that they participated in their religion, but it also seemed that the Second Temple period was the last time we really knew that God was listening.

Whether or not God was listening, in Jerusalem people were convinced God was still talking. The holy city was not kind to atheists; everybody believed something, and lived their lives accordingly. During the two years I spent in Jerusalem, I became more observant. It was easy to learn from the environment, and to live according to the rhythms of a traditional life. I embraced keeping kosher and celebrating the holidays and Shabbat.

The rabbis I studied with came from many points of view. But the ones I was drawn to the most thought about everything as if their lives depended on it. Small issues of kashrut and large issues of philosophy were debated with the same verve. Books flew off the shelves to take part in the conversations.

As much as I learned from the rabbis, a significant part of my learning had nothing to do with books and everything to do with cultural immersion. I rarely had the money to make Shabbat dinner in any significant way, and many people were kind enough to open their homes. Often when I was studying with someone, I would be asked to stay for dinner and I would offer to help in the kitchen, learning by doing. People are very forthcoming with their family recipes if you agree to cut and chop. It is thanks to those hours in the kitchen that I can cook a mean brisket, even though brisket is something I never had, growing up. I came from a tradition where cooking mattered and family recipes were sacrosanct, so I knew this learning, too, was essential. One of my teachers said to me: religion is guilt with different holidays and different food. Everybody eats. And even when they're not eating, they're still thinking about food.

My first Passover in Jerusalem, I joined my friends Michael and Jacob for a do-it-yourself seder. For me, new to Judaism, and for them, new to being away from their parents' homes, it was a first experience of making a seder. Michael and Jacob were in charge of the food, and, since I was vegetarian at the time, they wanted to make almond patties. As they started to make them, however, they noticed a strange smell. Some of the almonds were rotten. They decided to try each one before using it, sitting by the toilet and spitting the bad ones out. That is how you know your friends really care: if they are willing to risk cyanide poisoning for the sake of your meal. Later in the evening, I went outside to get some air, and almost collapsed under the weight of those patties. It was a night that one could only have in Jerusalem, with a group of friends, all at a certain age and stage of life. Passover lends itself to inquisitiveness; the rituals are all meant to make you ask questions. There is a teaching that even the table should be upside down for the seder, so that when guests walk in they begin by asking: Why? That night, we did everything and we talked about everything. It stands out as one of the best, most meaningful seders I have ever been privileged to attend.

The next day, I was invited to the home of a very prominent rabbi in Jerusalem, who was proud of the fact that I was coming over for one of my first seders. He wanted to show me and the other guests what a real seder could be. His family did not speak a lot of English, and I did not speak a lot of Hebrew. A bowl was passed around with a number of round objects that looked like matzah balls. I figured this was some tradition where the matzah balls were served separately from the soup. I was used to seeing matzah balls out of context, ever since the time my mother had decided to make matzah balls in black bean soup. Relatively speaking, the objects at the rabbi's table had more of a context; there was a garnish of carrots, and all that was missing was the broth. I bit into it. The slippery coldness and fishiness of my first bite was an unpleasant surprise. A taste for gefilte fish is not easy to acquire.

Gefilte fish aside, my commitment to Judaism grew deeper every day.

First Fruits

Finally, after years of study, I came before a *beit din*, a rabbinic court that officiated over conversions. One of my teachers spoke to the members on my behalf. They asked me questions, ranging from the ritual to the political. They wanted to know that I could keep a Jewish home and could pass down this fantastic gift that they were giving me. It was like organ donation: they were giving me something precious, they were giving me life, and they wanted to be sure I would put it to good use. To this day, I think of their decision to accept me as a *chesed shel emet*, an act of true kindness for which I can never express enough thanks.

Next came the mikvah, the ritual bath. In New York City, the mikvah of the Upper West Side is a luxury establishment. The walls are covered with breathtaking mosaics. There are individual changing rooms with baths and showers and luxurious robes, and, when you are ready to immerse, you discreetly push a button so the mikvah lady knows to come escort you to the pool. My experience at the mikvah in Israel was the exact opposite. As I was showering in preparation for the ritual immersion, the mikvah lady brusquely pulled the curtain aside to tell me I was done. It was like a moment out of a horror movie. I was both terrified and mortified, and I didn't know what to cover first. For a modest people, we have no problems demanding nakedness at moments of great holiness.

Standing in the mikvah, I was given a loose canvas bag to put over my body, and a small hat to go on my head, and the *beit din* came in. They started to yell at me. I was horrified. I had studied so hard for so long, I was living a *halakhic* life, what could possibly be wrong? I leaned closer to try to understand them, and the yelling only got louder, the gesticulations more wild. Was this some final hazing that I had failed to read about? Finally the mikvah lady started to make a motion with her hands, a combination of a turning gesture and something that looked like someone feeling melons. Through my tears I could make out what they were all saying: "*Sivuv! Sivuv!*"—that is, "Turn around! Turn around!" Suddenly I realized that the combination of the cloth and the water made for a wet tee-shirt moment, and they needed me to turn so that all they saw was my back. I quickly turned around and finished the prescribed ritual, including a formal renunciation of any previous religion. The beit din left, and I got out of the mikvah, not stopping to do anything except throw on my clothes. A picture taken soon after shows me standing in front of a bus stop, hair still wet, and grinning from ear to ear.

A week after the conversion, I became a bat mitzvah. It was a weekday morning at Pardes. The Torah portion was *Vayeshev*, the story of Joseph and his brothers. I led the service and read a small section of Torah—and came out to a surprise party. I was overwhelmed. There was even a cake with a dove on it, to celebrate my new Hebrew name. When I was growing up, my birthday, at the end of November, was always conflated with Thanksgiving; having my own party was a new experience. This and my wedding stand out as the two greatest celebrations I will ever have. Whenever I officiate at a conversion, I look back to this moment, and I can empathize with the range of emotions felt by my students.

As much as I was making a new beginning, my family ties followed me to Israel. Shortly after my conversion, my parents sent my former pastor, who was in Israel on a church trip, on a mission to get me back. This was the cool young pastor who had done missionary work in Papua, New Guinea, and told stories about being shot at by poison arrows. My parents knew him from our church in Hollis, Queens, where I had been baptized and where my father had been in charge of finances. When they left Queens and moved to the church on Long Island, they got involved in the pastoral search committee and, because of them, he was hired.

My mother, despite her stated support for my new religious path, had hopes that I would return to the fold. Hearing that the pastor was leading a trip to Israel, she gave him my schedule and contact information. He called me at the yeshiva and said, "Let's meet for dinner. It's a Saturday night and I know that you're off." He took me out to an expensive kosher dairy restaurant. It was a classic American-in-Israel experience; he ordered from every part of the menu, a five-course meal. It had been a long time since I had had a meal with more than one course. Actually, it had been a long time since I had had a meal made up of more than falafel. He realized at the end of the meal that he had forgotten his wallet. Fortunately, I had just done a house cleaning job and had cash in my pocket. I needed it for rent, but I used it to pay the bill. He seemed shocked that I had the money to cover this, but I did not want to tell him where it was from: he would go home and tell my parents I had gone from being a Protestant pre-med student to a Middle Eastern maid, and I knew that such a conversation would not end well. Religious identity was one thing. Cleaning strangers' bathrooms was another.

The pastor had spent the meal talking about how wonderful Israel was, and how exciting it was to travel to all the places that Jesus had been. I had been spending the past year and a half getting excited about going to all the places that Jesus was not. We really did not have a lot to say to each other.

My parents had tried something similar the previous summer, when I went home between my two years at Pardes. One night at dinner, I was surprised to see their pastor at the table. After the meal, they left the two of us alone. I got the sense that the pastor did not want to spend one of his evenings going to his parishioners' home for dinner and a pastoral visit to bring their Jewish lesbian daughter back to the fold. In Hollis, this man had invigorated an aging church, but, by the time he got to the suburbs, the ministry was taking its toll. He cut to the chase and said, "Look, your parents want to make sure you're okay. Are you feeling manipulated?" "I didn't until now," I replied. He seemed satisfied with that answer. "You'll be one of my new Jewish friends," he said. By the end of our conversation, I had him trying on a tallit and tefillin. It was not surprising, then, that when he saw me in Israel he did not expect me to change.

That spring, I observed my first Passover as a full-fledged Jew, and seven weeks later I celebrated Shavuot. Shavuot is a special festival for converts, for two reasons. First, it is the time that we read the Book of Ruth. Ruth was the paradigmatic convert, leaving everything she knew to follow her mother-in-law Naomi, and to choose the Jewish God. Second, it is the time we celebrate having received the Torah at Mount Sinai. Our tradition teaches that every Jew, whether present in the desert or not, whether born Jewish or not, was standing there at Sinai, hearing God's word and accepting the Torah. It is a journey that begins with coming out of Egypt, continues through the desert, and leads to the mountain.

As I look back on my own journey, I think of one of the Passover prayers, *Dayenu*, "It would have been enough for us." This is a mirror image of the response a convert is meant to give when asked whether he or she is aware of what it means to join the Jewish people, given the persecution and suffering we have endured. The convert is meant to reply "I know, and I am not worthy—*eini kedai*." I am not worthy, none of us are worthy, and yet we find our way. Dayenu— it is enough. The individual ("I am not worthy") is transformed into the communal ("It would have been enough for us"). I am so grateful to be part of this people.

Perhaps the worth of any individual is dwarfed by the hardships of history. Then again, perhaps the only way we become worthy is by moving forward together. Eini kedai,

I am not worthy, transforms into a collective Dayenu. If we can look back on what we have done and say "Dayenu," we realize it is enough.

Even if I had only left what I knew was a lie: It would have been enough.

Even if I only had the privilege of living and studying in Jerusalem and not become a rabbi: It would have been enough.

Even if I had only dreamed of having daughters to carry on this blessing and never had the strength to pull it off: It would have been enough.

Even if I had found only a moment of the love and joy I have in my life, and never found my place in this world: It would have been enough.

That I can do more each day is without measure.

The *Treyfa* Banquet

Funerals in the New York City area can require a lot of driving. Some of the Jewish cemeteries are in Suffolk County, on the east end of Long Island, over an hour's drive from Manhattan. After officiating one day at such a far-flung funeral, I pulled into a Dunkin' Donuts to get some caffeine to propel myself home. Before getting out of the car, I took off my kippah and left it beside my *Rabbi's Manual* on the front passenger seat. As I headed in for coffee, I happened to glance into the car immediately to the right of my own. On the front passenger seat, there was a kippah and a *Rabbi's Manual*. I smiled, and went inside. I did not know who the car belonged to, but I knew I had a colleague nearby. For a moment, both of us were taking off our rabbi hats, and getting some sustenance for the long drive home.

Often, the meals we choose are simply sustenance: they are a means to an end. "Without bread, there is no Torah," the rabbis taught, "and without Torah, there is no bread"

(Pirkei Avot 3:21). Other times, a meal says something more. In my family, the ability to cook was prized. From the time I was a young girl, my grandmother would explain to me that, if you couldn't make a good sauce, you couldn't make anything, but if you *could* make a good sauce, you could get through years of a marriage and no one would know any better. The way she saw it, good cooking could hide a multitude of sins. It was a way to express love, and a way to get out of trouble.

Sometimes, meals get you out of trouble—and sometimes meals get you into trouble. A few years ago, I made a pilgrimage to Cincinnati, the historical heartland of American Reform Judaism. I wanted to go to the archives, to see the original menu for the Treyfa Banquet. In the summer of 1883, a formal dinner was held at the Highland House restaurant in Cincinnati. It was part of the celebration surrounding the ordination of four American rabbis from the Hebrew Union College. These were the first American rabbis ordained at an American seminary, under the leadership of Rabbi Isaac Mayer Wise. Wise is known as the founder of the institutions of American Reform Judaism, but his vision was more inclusive; he wanted to be part of the creation of a pluralistic American Judaism.

The banquet played a part in the disappearance of that dream. With Jews and non-Jews of all denominations in attendance, the food was served. It was full of nonkosher delicacies, including clams, frogs' legs, and lobsters, along with milk mixed with meat. There has been much debate about who approved the menu, and whether in fact those who had seen it would have found it problematic. From the perspective of normative Cincinnati Judaism, it might have been seen as respectful of Jewish law because the menu omitted pork. But to other Jews in attendance, it was an insult. The dinner became a flashpoint for the denominational divide that has characterized American Judaism ever since.

Everyone can find a reason to object to someone else. At the same conference where Lisa and I met in Germany, two other conference-goers met and fell in love. She was a Turkish Muslim, and he was a British Muslim. They faced as much opposition from their families for being a "mixed marriage" as we did for being gay.

One of my favorite stories is of two rabbis who were about to enter Caesarea, a Jewish town notorious for the bad behavior of its inhabitants. One said to the other, "Why are we entering this place that is filled with blasphemers?" The other got off his donkey, picked up sand from the ground, and stuffed it in the first rabbi's mouth. Once he could speak, the first rabbi—not unreasonably—asked, "Why did you do that?" "Because," the other rabbi replied, "God is displeased with the one who denounces Israel."

One of the greatest lessons I learned at the Academy for Jewish Religion was that, at the end of the day, we have a lot to learn from one another. The most articulate description of the rabbinate that I have ever encountered is infused with this belief. This description was initially taught to me by Rabbi Bernard Zlotowitz, one of my first teachers at the Academy. He quoted from an ordination essay written by Rabbi Nehemiah Anton Nobel, an Orthodox rabbi born in Hungary in 1874. Upon his ordination, Rabbi Nobel was asked what mission a rabbi should seek to fulfill. He stated:

> I hold that a rabbi can fulfill his task successfully only if he stands above all parties within and outside his community. He himself must have a firm and unflinching standpoint—one not given to appeals—on all the religious issues of his time. . . . But, I consider it my duty to examine every religious trend within Judaism, to meet it with objective arguments only, and to treat the representatives of opposition movements and viewpoints with the kind of respect we owe to ardent oppo-

nents. I want to lay greater stress in my public activities on that which unites different trends than on those
causes which separate them. . . . This is my ideal of the
rabbi as I see it, and to strive for its realization is my
life's task.

Denominations are only the current configurations of
something that existed long before, and will exist long after.
If you want to see the most historically accurate picture of
denominationalism, watch Monty Python's movie *The Life
of Brian*. We have always argued, we have always configured
and reconfigured ourselves in different ways, and ultimately
we are all in the same boat. One thing I have noticed about
the Jewish community is that everyone feels on the margin.
This is only possible if the true shape of the Jewish people
is a mobius bagel, with no real inner side, just a lot of folks
on the outside of a continuum.

All the same, the Treyfa Banquet marked a significant
moment, and it looked far tastier than a bagel. I wanted to
see the menu. I had seen replicas, and I was intrigued both
by the issues of kashrut and the issues of fine dining. A French
friend who has her grandmother's cookbook from the 1920s
researched all of the courses and concluded that not only was
there significant mangling of French grammar and spelling,
but the French rules for the proper order of a meal had been
broken. Apparently this is no laughing matter. In her words,
"It's like opening the door for Elijah at the beginning of the
seder and concluding with the *mah nishtanah*." The menu
seemed a bungled attempt to be both Jewishly sensitive and
culturally impressive. For most people in attendance, it
probably succeeded. The local newspapers record that it
was a lovely affair. Fallout aside, I imagine many of the
attendees went home full and happy.

I knew it would make a difference to see the menu with
my own eyes. A few years earlier, I had accompanied Lisa to

Cambridge University. She wanted to see original fragments from the Cairo Geniza, medieval Hebrew documents relevant to her dissertation. We made a trip of it, using the opportunity to look through antiquarian bookstores, punt down the river, reflect on the virtues of Oxford over its rival, and take a tour which began at a church with the most Aryan stained-glass Jesus either of us had ever seen. The highlight of the trip, for her, was the Geniza. She needed a special letter of permission to be allowed into the room where the fragments were kept, and she emerged ecstatic. It was not that she had discovered something new; she was simply moved by having come in direct contact with these writings, words from our ancestors over a thousand years ago.

That was how I felt about wanting to see the menu from the Treyfa Banquet. I planned a road trip from New York to Cincinnati. It would be my first time away from home since Ariella had been born, four years before. Two days before my intended departure, Lisa asked whether I needed anything sent to the dry cleaners, and I asked her to send my peacoat so I would be warm in the cold Cincinnati spring. She was kind enough to do so, but busy enough that she did not check the pockets. As soon as we realized that my wallet was inside, we called the dry cleaners, who claimed to know nothing about it. We were rabbinic enough to want to give the benefit of the doubt, and New Yorkers enough to be skeptical. We went that night to the premises and found the remains of my wallet in a garbage bag outside the cleaners. My business cards, receipts, and photographs were all there; my credit cards, driver's license, and money were not. I had been cleaned out by the cleaners.

It was a tough turn-around, but I managed to get a replacement license in just enough time to save the trip. My time in the archives was interrupted with calls from the police detective on the case, who conceded that it did rise to the level of a felony. Ultimately, though, it did not rank high enough compared to other crimes in the Bronx. What mattered was that I made it to Cincinnati.

This was not the first time I'd lost my wallet in connection with a significant Jewish journey. At Brandeis, I met the woman who was to become my first serious girlfriend. Susie had two qualities that, though I didn't realize it at the time, would soon form a pattern in my life. She was Jewish, and she was Canadian. She also happened to be very, very athletic. She was an avid runner and a member of the varsity soccer team. Fitness was a part of who she was, and I wanted nothing so much as to impress her. She asked me to meet her family in Montreal, and we made plans to go there over the semester break in December. On the way, we would stop in Lake George and do what she referred to as "ice camping." Now, this did not seem right to me; my mother had taught me that nature was a malevolent force, best domesticated or ignored. The family saying was "If it doesn't flush, we don't go."

I had no equipment, and I didn't want to show my ignorance by asking what I might need. I went out and bought a pair of Timberlands, which seemed like serious gear at the time. The truth was, Susie had never really gone ice camping herself. She was outfitted in Nike boots, with no crampons, and no weather gear. Looking back, she probably wanted to impress me, as well.

And so it was that I drove my Camaro Z28 to Lake George, where there was three feet of snow. Even to drive to the beginning of the trail was tough, but we made it. Attempting to hike to the tent area was the real challenge. Within minutes, we hit a very narrow part of the path, which ran over sixty feet above the edge of a river. Beside us was a sheer drop, wet ground sparsely dotted with trees and rocks. I again mentioned that I did not think that this was a great idea, and, as had happened all the other times, she ignored me. She was too intrepid and too full of Canadian can-do to think this might be a mistake. According to Lisa, there is a particular combination of an inferiority complex and a superiority complex that many Canadians carry, and it can sometimes lead to unwise decisions. "You'll be fine," Susie assured me. "Stop being such an American chicken."

The moment she uttered those words, I slipped, sliding feet-first and face-down along the side of the cliff. I had fallen three or four feet when my right foot hit a stump. It was far enough, and Susie was short enough, that she could not reach me. My backpack plummeted as I struggled to regain my nonexistent balance. Susie wrenched a branch off the side of a tree and extended it to me. The presence of this branch was like one of those miracles that Maimonides writes about. He posits that certain things existed from the beginning of creation, waiting for their moment to be of use. Had it not been for this stick and her impressive upper body strength, I would have been dead. I pulled myself up, entirely covered in mud. Everything in my backpack was gone: my books and maps, my wallet, and my clothes. For some reason, my car keys and passport were in the pocket of my cargo pants; they were the only items still in my possession. Their presence there was a rare piece of luck, because it is very hard to hotwire a Camaro, and I didn't want to have to show off (and explain) that particular skill so early in the relationship. We turned around, trudged back to the car, and continued our drive north to Montreal. When we reached her home in Côte St. Luc, a fancy Jewish suburb, and I met her parents, I was still clad in cargo pants and covered in mud. From the top of my purple faux-hawk to the bottom of my grimy Timberlands, I must have been a sight to behold. I was the first girl Susie had ever brought home.

A few months later, back at Brandeis, I was shocked to receive my backpack in the mail. Everything was in it, down to the cash in my wallet. Some poor ranger had written a note saying "I hope that you're okay when you get this, and that you had a safe journey out of the park." I could imagine the ranger's fear that he might be sending the package to a dead person, or that the living would sue.

By the time I received the backpack, the romance had long since worn off. I had come out to my parents about being gay and wanting to convert, and had made the decision to go to Israel. The ID in the wallet was still mine, but who I was had changed. I was different, but only because I was becoming more of myself. It was then that I started to articulate what guided my own journey, as well as the principle I use to guide others: any major life change should only make you more of who you are.

The trip to Cincinnati confirmed for me that I had made another of those changes: I had become a Reform Jew. Like Lisa with the fragments from the Geniza, when I held the menu from the Treyfa Banquet, I felt a connection that transcended time and space. These were my people, and here was my history.

The menu itself was smaller than I expected, decorated with peacock feathers, on ivory paper, and written in a beautiful art-deco font. For all the misspelled French and misplaced courses, it was clearly an example of food as an act of grace. It reminded me of nothing so much as *Babette's Feast*. This meal was meant to bring joy, to dazzle all those in attendance with the best that Cincinnati had to offer, and with American Judaism as well. I looked at the menu, so small and so beautiful, and thought of Helen of Troy. How could something so delicate and elegant have been the cause of so much trouble?

My own journey took me from learning how to keep a kosher kitchen, to my pilgrimage to see the menu of the Treyfa Banquet. Along the way, my Jewish practice changed. Even before I was Jewish, I did not eat much nonkosher food. Pork always smelled like a biology experiment, and I avoided it at all costs. As for seafood, my brother has an iodine allergy, so anytime I saw shellfish I would think, "Maybe this one's the killer." For many years, I was vegetarian, and that became a big part of my kashrut. Years before anyone was talking about carbon footprints, not eating meat was part of my deal with God: I did not want to hurt any living being, and I wanted to have a positive impact on the world. When I started eating meat for health reasons, living in Israel made keeping kosher feel natural. In Jerusalem, one must go out of the way to find treyf. As I cleaned houses and *kashered* kitchens, I learned to love the rigor of kashrut, especially with the added stringencies of the shemitta year. There was something very special to watching what you put in your mouth, and to feeling that the land is sustaining you.

The years I spent in Jerusalem, I lived a traditional life, and I cherished it. I wish that modern Israel was a place where I could live and work as a liberal lesbian rabbi and be happy and embraced, but it's not. Perhaps one day it will be, and on that day I will very happily return, and sit around the Shabbat table with my friends once more. But I had to leave Israel to continue on my path, and, when I did, I entered a different world and a different life. And, when I entered rabbinical school, the more I learned, the more I realized that differences of opinion and local customs have always played a part when it comes to Judaism and personal choice. The laws of Passover food vary based on whether you are of Eastern European or Spanish Jewish origins, from Ashkenaz or Sepharad. Even the Mishnah has a minority opinion that would permit chicken parmesan.

It seems to me that our Reform ancestors need not have been so apologetic in the wake of the Treyfa Banquet. They were following their own local custom, their own *minhag ha-makom*. Should how we eat at one another's events and in one another's homes constantly be modified to defer to the practices of those who are more traditional? That said, I still have three sets of dishes—one dairy, one meat, one treyf—because I care very much about my friends being comfortable. And, unlike those early Reform Jews who derided "kitchen Judaism," from both my Jewish family and my family of origin I know how much food matters. I still follow my own brand of kashrut. My pregnancy was the only exception. Lisa and I joke that Ariella is a good 15 percent Slim Jims. The crowning moment, though, came during my second trimester. I had a craving for seafood and steak. We went to a restaurant, where I eagerly ordered an appetizer of king crab legs, and a prime rib for the main course. When it came time for dessert, I wanted more crab legs. Embarrassed, I asked Lisa to order them for me. She is more of a traditionalist than I am, when it comes to keeping kosher, so it was a true sign of love when she asked the waitress for an order of crab legs for dessert. With a strained smile, she accepted the bowl and the nutcracker used to crack the shell and extract the meat. She even put on the plastic bib, emblazoned with a bright red crab. As soon as the waitress turned away, I grabbed the crab legs and started eating them. The bib shielded Lisa from the onslaught of shell and butter as the legs piled up in the metal bowl, a treyfa banquet of my very own. Lisa had the crème brulee.

In my own life and practice, I have increasingly realized how much there is a connection between politics and the modern practice of kashrut. I have a real concern about supporting a system of food certification operated by those who would rather I did not exist. I have no illusions that the same people who determine whether meat is kosher would deny the legitimacy of my rabbinate and my family. But Judaism is not a democracy; at best, it's a broken socialism. So I don't impose my philosophy on others, much as I hope others will not impose their philosophies on me.

I feel blessed to know the joy of sitting with friends around a Shabbat table, singing songs and eating Shabbat foods and talking about the Torah portion; I feel lucky to know from the inside what it means to live a traditional life. Once, in an intradenominational encounter, an earnest modern Orthodox rabbinical student asked if I missed living a traditional Jewish life. "Do you feel as if your life is crippled," he asked me, "living outside of *halakhah*?" I thought about his question, then I thought about the work I have done in congregational life, the people I have served, the people who depend on me to show up, and the role I play in the Jewish life of a community as a rebbetzin as well as a rabbi. I thought of all the things I could not do, and all the people I could not reach, if I lived only within the boundaries of halakhah. "No," I told him, "I am not halakhically crippled. I am just differently halakhically abled. I can do more with less."

I am not a ritual girl. I do not need to keep kosher or keep Shabbat in a traditional way to feel that God is close to me, or that I am part of the Jewish people. That is the gift of classical Reform Judaism. Wearing a kippah does not make me any more or less a Jew than would eating a piece of pork. But I would live or die for a people that may not want me anyway, and I know every day that I am the leader of something that is real and true and alive, something that will outlast me, and something that will survive anything that comes against it. I do believe that we are an eternal people and our task in the world is to be better to others than they are to us, no matter what the circumstances. We do this because the one God commands us, and the language of that commandment, for me, is Judaism. That it isn't, for some others, is fine with me, but for me Judaism is the best way to hear that commandment, with the least interference and the least need for translation. Whatever is on my plate, I know that I am a Jew.

If I have learned anything from integrating my Jewish identity with my non-Jewish family, it is that there is a way for people to coexist. If this is true of Jews and non-Jews, then it ought to be true of Jews with one another; there just needs to be some combination of compassion and having a thick skin. I imagine Jewish communal life to be like the clichéd Olive Garden family, but dysfunctional and real. You are sitting around a big table with all your relatives, distant and close. They get it wrong, more often than not, but the effort is appreciated. There will be critical parents, the siblings no one talks about, and cousins who look down their noses. You sometimes have to force your way to the food, and not be daunted if someone throws it. Once you have a seat, it's yours; you just have to make your way to the table. We do not need to agree in order to sit down together, and we should have no illusions that it will be easy. But it will be worthwhile. Bring all of who you are to the table and see what happens. I would suggest avoiding the gefilte fish, but there is debate about this, as well.

11

Tisha B'Av

Broken Sound

You shall sound a broken blast on the shofar, in the seventh month, on the tenth day of the month—the Day of Atonement—you shall have the shofar sounded throughout your land.

—Leviticus 25:9

Fore!giveness: An Introduction

As someone who looks more like a German tourist than a stereotypical rabbi, I am rarely what people expect to see. This came home to me when I was preparing to lead my first High Holiday Services. After traveling through a hurricane to get from New York to Boca Raton for my first pulpit as a student rabbi, I waited at the airport for the congregant assigned to meet me. Someone who matched the description I had been given entered the baggage area, and briskly walked right by me. I watched as she asked everyone else on the flight whether he or she was the rabbi. Eventually, I caught up with her and told her I was the rabbi. "Really?" she asked, looking me up and down. "Nice to meet you. Let's get your rental car." It was a white Bronco, O.J. style. Now, that got me noticed. I was pulled over three times in the course of two days.

As I checked into the hotel, one other thing got me noticed: my shofar, the long, spiraled antelope horn used on Rosh Hashanah. As the person behind the desk checked me in, the hotel manager passed by and smiled. His polite greeting morphed into quiet whiplash as he turned to see the long object peeking out of my bag.

What started out as cordial curiosity spiraled into great concern. Our exchange continued cautiously:

"My, what a large object you have there," the manager said. It occurred to me that this long shofar looked a bit like a gun. "Yes, it's an occupational hazard." "And what exactly is it that you do?" "I'm a rabbi. All I need is my room, a way to print my sermon, and a place to practice this shofar. It's a ritual object, nothing harmful." He took a moment to collect himself, and put his game face back on. Then he assured me that he would do everything he could to make me comfortable, but asked that I not practice in his hotel. "Surely," he said, "the golf course behind the hotel would be more appropriate."

So it was that the next morning, I was outside with my shofar on the Broken Sound Golf Club. The night before, Erev Rosh Hashanah, I had led the overflow service in a seafoam-green school auditorium. For this service, the congregation flew me in as their student rabbi, and bused in the elderly and the deaf. They were also trying to attract young Floridians, an elusive demographic, with a singles service planned for Rosh Hashanah afternoon. I had slept soundly in the hotel, thousands of miles away from any family members who might want to drop in with pots and pans. Waking up bright and early, I went to the golf course to practice the shofar before returning to the synagogue to lead the morning service.

I figured I would have the course to myself. It was, after all, early in the morning on the first day of Rosh Hashanah in Boca Raton. But, as it turned out, I was not alone, as I discovered when a golf ball winged me on the head. I awoke bleeding and dazed. Fortunately, the ball had only nicked the back of my right ear; if it had hit me straight on, I would be dead. The first thing I could focus on was a large gold *chai* necklace, featuring the Hebrew word for life, poking through a puff of white chest hair. Morris, my assailant, was in his late sixties, and he had come for an early round of golf. He was mortified at having hit me, and his embarrassment only increased when he saw the shofar. I told him who I was, and why I was on the golf course. When I mentioned the name of the temple where I was leading services, he cringed. It was clear that he had decided to come to the Broken Sound Golf Course instead of hearing the sound of the shofar this Rosh Hashanah, and he had certainly not expected to find both in the same place. He helped me back into the hotel, and brought a wet cloth, which I held to my head.

As I tried to collect myself, he told me his story. It was a phenomenon I would become increasingly familiar with as a rabbinical student and, later, as a rabbi. Whenever I tell someone what I do, whether it's sitting in an airplane or concussed on a golf course, they tell me about their Jewish lives. "I'm not a good Jew. I haven't been to temple in years," he confessed, "not since my son died." He went on to describe how he had been divorced for over thirty years, and his son had been not only his golf partner but his only family and closest friend. He hadn't had the desire to find someone to play golf with after his son had died, and he certainly had no desire to go to synagogue, to pray to a God who had taken his beloved son too soon. He wouldn't go back there, not even to drop off a rabbi whom he had hit on the head with a golf ball.

I listened with new ears to his story, as the ones I had were swelling and ringing. I felt a small bit of blood oozing down the right side of my head. The concussion actually honed my listening skills, and kept me quiet, which is key to any chaplaincy situation. I think it was the first time he had actually felt heard. We said our goodbyes. I went to my room, cleaned up, found my way to my white Bronco, and drove myself to the synagogue. I had a few minutes to collect myself before the service, and made it through without a hitch. Even though I had years of education ahead of me, this was my first Rosh Hashanah as a rabbi. I was concussed, but I was clergy.

The Road to Rosh Hashanah

The time leading up to the High Holidays begins weeks before. A significant stopping point along the way is Tisha B'Av, the ninth day of the summer month of Av, when we remember the destruction of both Temples, and mourn other tragedies in our past. It can be hard, sometimes even impossible, to move past Tisha B'Av. But, as the rabbis of the Talmud taught, someone who mourns too much for one thing actually is mourning something else.

The story is told of four rabbis who entered Pardes. Pardes is the name of the yeshiva where I studied for my two years in Jerusalem, but the word itself is an acronym for four levels of interpreting the Torah: *Pshat* (the plain meaning), *Remez* (the meanings that are alluded to), *Drash* (the deeper interpretation), and *Sod* (the secret, or mystical, meanings). However, the earliest meaning of the word is *paradise*, and that is the meaning with which this story begins.

> The rabbis taught: Four [sages] entered Pardes. They were Ben Azzai, Ben Zoma, Acher, and Rabbi Akiva. Rabbi Akiva said to them, "When you arrive at the slabs of pure transparent marble, do not say, 'Water! Water!' for it is said, 'He who speaks untruths shall not stand before My eyes' (Psalms 101:7)." Ben Azzai looked and died. Regarding him the verse states, "Precious in the sight of the Eternal is the death of God's saints" (Psalms 116:15). Ben Zoma looked and went mad. Regarding him the verse states, "Did you find honey? Eat only as much as you need, lest you be overfilled and vomit it

up" (Proverbs 25:16). Acher cut down the plantings
[that is, he left his religion]. Rabbi Akiva left in peace.

—Babylonian Talmud (Chagigah 14b),
Zohar (I, 26b), and
Tikunei Zohar (Tikun 40)

Ben Azzai looked and died; Ben Zoma looked and went
mad; Acher looked and left religion; Akiva entered and left
in peace, and didn't look back. Grief makes more sense
when we divide it into stages, or attach different reactions
to different people. As in "She's going through denial" or "He
never shows how he feels." But grief doesn't make sense. All
of these stages and each of these characters are aspects of the
same self. Each of the sages is looking at the same thing, and
each experiences all of the reactions. What matters is where
they end up.

Ben Azzai Looked and Died

When I walked into Pardes, I saw beautiful young
people, learning beautiful old things. There was a shared generosity, and an eagerness to experience everything that a year
in Jerusalem could offer. I had keys to the building, because
my late nights often outlasted the teachers'. More than
once, I was found the next morning, face down in a text from
the night before.

For many of us, this was our first excursion from home.
Some had been to Israel before, but this was the first time
we had lived there independently. At the time, Pardes was
in a brand-new building, still establishing itself, and one had
to find one's own apartment. Now there is a concierge service, which must be worth its weight in gold.

Many of us studied and prayed at a number of places, to
round out our experience. We wanted to explore everything
we could. For most of us, this was a year or two of intellec-
tual and spiritual discovery. We were not tourists, but the

majority of us were not looking to live and die in Israel. And yet some stayed to live, and some died.

I always felt safe in Jerusalem, as if I could sleep on the streets. Even when bad things happened, they felt very compartmentalized, much as they do in New York City: if something doesn't happen in your neighborhood, it soon becomes yesterday's news. The first year I was there, a group of Israeli army women came to speak to the students at Pardes. They were beautiful, each eighteen years old, with Uzis slung over their shoulders and perfectly tight shirts. I was inspired, to say the least, and paid close attention to their presentation. They were talking about how safe Israel was in comparison with other parts of the world, and they mentioned that there had been a shooting just that day near New York City. I had a bad feeling. People get shot *in* New York City all the time, but the minute you say "near New York City," that means the suburbs—more unusual and, in my case, closer to home. We found out within an hour or two that there had been a shooting at the train stop by my house. Some lunatic had stood up on the 5:33 rush hour commuter train to Port Jefferson, pulled out a gun, and started shooting. Six people were killed, and nineteen were injured. My father could have easily been on this train—and he has a history of getting shot. The soldiers' lesson hit home. The most dangerous thing that ever happened in my neighborhood high school was a fight with a plastic fork, and now there were multiple murders on the local train. I imagined what these young soldiers would have done the moment the shooter got on the train. Then I imagined what would have happened if the train had been filled with Israelis, with everyone who was over fifteen and under eighty ready and able to stop the murders.

Despite the fact that Israel felt like the safest place in the world, the reality of where we were living came home. My first year there, I really wanted to participate and contribute in any way I could. Rhea suggested that I join the Mishmar, the volunteer police. They were very amused to see a naïve-looking American woman showing up as a recruit. They took me to the firing range, to teach me and the other recruits how to use firearms. The first time, the recoil almost knocked my teeth out, and the Israelis looked at me and laughed. But within a few minutes, they stopped laughing. Thanks to many, many years playing video games, I was a dead shot—and did three or four bulls' eyes in a row. I was a card-carrying member after that.

I entered Pardes, and I looked. Among the many people I saw there, I found two who were a couple and my friends. Matt and Sara were like salt and pepper shakers; small, brilliant, and beautiful, they were a perfect match. He was a wrestler from Yale and she was an environmental activist from Barnard. They really looked as if God had made them for each other, and that is not a phrase I use lightly.

It was Purim at Pardes. Sara was chanting the *megillah*, the Scroll of Esther, which tells the story of the holiday. Everyone was busy being earnest and keeping their eyes on their own texts, to keep up with her flawless chanting. It was only when someone looked up that we saw: as Sara was reading the section about Vashti, Achashverosh's first wife who refused to dance for him unclothed, she herself was slowly taking her clothes off, waiting to see if anyone would notice. It was a classic Purim moment.

While Sara was reading the megillah in Jerusalem, Baruch Goldstein, a Jewish extremist, killed almost thirty Arabs praying in a mosque in Hebron. Two years later, again near Purim, Matt and Sara were murdered in a revenge killing, when the bus they were on was blown up. All my friends from Pardes—including Matt—were in the second year of their rabbinical studies, back in Israel. I was the only one from our group who was in New York, the only one present when their bodies were brought home. There were so many people who were so much closer to them, but the context in which I knew them was very special. The parents of one of my friends from Israel gave me a lift to the funeral; for them, this was as close as they could get to being there with their son. I was a very young person, with the very big weight of wishing there was more I could do.

I watched a packed house at their funerals, and I watched them being buried. The funerals began in Teaneck, New Jersey, and continued in Hartford, Connecticut, one right after the other. There was a convoy of cars that went on forever, traveling to the gravesites, together outside of Hartford. Matt and Sara were so young yet they had affected so many people. When I think of them, I think of a Midrash on Aaron's sons, Nadav and Avihu, who were consumed by fire at the height of their youth. The point, the Midrash teaches, is not how they died, but how they lived. And then I think of the passage from the Talmud that Matt taught near the end of his life, and that is on the wall of a study hall dedicated in the couple's memory, "Study is greater than action, for study leads to action." The tragedy is in how much more study, and how much more action, they could have accomplished in their lives. They were the best of us, and they are gone.

I did not know it at the time, but many people from the Academy for Jewish Religion, the place where I would study to become a rabbi, were also there. These were people who would one day become my colleagues, people whom I would come to know and respect. One day, I too would lead Jewish communities at moments of loss, but, on that day, I was simply grieving. Bohr's model of the atom involves concentric rings of electrons. Each ring has two electrons going in opposite directions; we cannot ever know exactly where they are, but we know that they exist. Our lives hold within them opposite possibilities at any given moment. Stay in Israel or return to America; step on a bus or step off; have the opportunity to pursue your dream, or lose it. In the blink of an eye, in the explosion of a bomb, our direction can change. Had my path been slightly different, I could have been on that bus. Part of me moved forward from the day of Matt and Sara's funerals. Part of me looked, and died.

Ben Zoma Looked and Went Mad

A few months later, I went to buy plane tickets, to return to Israel for the first time since Matt and Sara had died. It took a lot to go in to the travel agent; I was still traumatized by their deaths, and nervous about going back. The travel agent was a woman named Maria, who worked with my mother in the medical office but was moonlighting in travel. Walking out, ticket in hand, I looked up into the sky. It was too early to see a shooting star in summer. But a shooting star was what I thought I saw; I knew that something was wrong. Driving home, I noticed that everyone had their windows rolled down and was listening to the news. "How Israeli," I thought to myself, and turned on the radio. A plane had taken off from JFK airport, full of people headed for Paris: TWA Flight 800. It had exploded over the ocean, and the water off Long Island was full of dead people and gasoline and luggage. The immediate assumption was that this had been a terrorist act. I thought immediately of Matt and Sara and how they had been killed.

The next day, my neighbor came to the door. He and his wife were a lovely, elderly couple, and he and my grandfather had been best friends for years. He told me that some of his family members had been on this flight, people I had grown up with. He knew that I was about to start studying to become a rabbi, and, even though he himself was not Jewish, clergy was clergy. He asked for my help. He knew that they were dead, but he wanted me to find them.

I had no idea what to do. I only knew that I wanted to help. I couldn't be there for Matt and Sara, and so I wanted to be there for my neighbor. There was no way I could look him in the face and say no. So I called the morgue on Veterans' Highway that was receiving the bodies, and described the situation to the man who answered the phone. "Please come," he said, "all the rabbis and other clergy are at JFK taking care of the families." So I went to the morgue. When I got there, I found myself alongside a woman from the Salvation Army, and a reverend who worked with the FBI. We sat in a small room, adjacent to the morgue. The head of the investigation was a Jewish dentist, and when he found out there was someone Jewish, he asked me to come to the back and say kaddish. I told him about my neighbor and his family, and asked if I could look for them. "Yes," he said, "come and look." And so I did.

When I walked into that room, I walked from my Long Island world to the front of a war zone. At Brandeis, I had worked as an EMT, and I certainly had seen death before. But this was different. These people, whose remains I saw that day, knew that they were going to die. Most were unrecognizable, but fear was on their faces, and their anger filled the air. I saw rings with fingers still attached, and I saw bodies sewn back together with thick black thread, but I could not find my neighbor's family. There was nothing I could do except what I was asked, and so I did: I said a prayer.

I know now that I never should have been there. In New York on 9/11, when rabbinic students stepped up to serve, no one was allowed on site who had not been specially trained. The day that TWA Flight 800 crashed, I had not even begun my studies. I was young, like a soldier jumping into battle. I thought I could do anything. I just wanted to serve, for all the right intentions. Someone asked and I said yes.

As a rabbi, it is important to acknowledge the mistakes that you make. Forgive my arrogance and my chutzpah, my lack of foresight and wisdom, all of which were subsumed under wanting to do the right thing. It is so hard to do the right thing, especially when there isn't much to guide you except your instincts and some faith. These do not always guide us well. On some level, after what I saw that day, I felt chased by the spirits of the people who were there, as if they wanted to kill me for being where I should not have been, for seeing things I should not have seen. But mostly they were mad at me because there was nothing I could do, and because I was not good enough to bear witness to their pain.

And so I carried into rabbinical school my own take on biblical criticism. Instead of the documentary hypothesis, which posits four sources—J, E, P, and D—I brought four different sources: P, T, S, and D. Post-Traumatic Stress Disorder. I left that morgue with a desperate need for light. I would go into electric-lighting stores just to look at bulbs and attachments. I slept with the lights on for two years. I had no health insurance, and I came from a culture that did not believe in therapy. And so I did the best I could. The brain is an incredible thing, constantly moving, trying to heal itself, reliving traumas to imagine them better. Maybe this time it will be different . . . except it never is. The smell of gasoline and sea water and death will never leave my mind.

My neighbor asked me to look. The head of the investigation said that I could look. I looked, and I went mad.

Acher Looked, and Left His Religion

When our other friends were still watching *Sesame Street*, my best friend Jeannie and I watched horror movies. I was raised on this genre, seeing the endless ways human bodies can be destroyed. Until that day in the morgue, I had no idea how accurate these movies actually were. Jeannie lived next door to a mortician, who sometimes kept bodies in the garage. From an early age, we knew that death was a reality, but it was a reality that somehow was not real. Halloween was our favorite holiday. We grew up in a time of suburban fears of pins in candy, a time of poisoned apples. My mother designated herself the official taster for all our loot, so we developed a strategy to eat as we went. We would sneak candy while dodging bricks in socks swung by neighborhood boys, and the occasional rotten egg. Death was not real, and we would live forever.

In high school science, I accidentally put a scalpel through the webbing of my left hand. It bled for hours. On the walk home with Jeannie, that day, I decided to conceal it until we passed a white wall. Maximizing the effect, I undid the bandage and sprayed my blood against the wall. Jeannie screamed. It was life imitating art, and we thought it was hilarious.

Jeannie and I don't watch horror movies anymore. We are older and we know better. And violence is not something I ever take for granted. But I still love my video games, and I am still a great shot. I keep playing and replaying the script in my mind, trying to find a different ending.

Sometimes, you almost think you have found one. I was in Israel when the peace treaty was signed between Yasser Arafat and Yitzhak Rabin. I bought a newspaper that day, as did everybody else, with the hope that it would become more than just a footnote in history. People stood in line for this paper as if it were a lottery ticket for a multimillion-dollar jackpot. The newsstands raised the prices, but, whatever it cost, it was worth it. It felt so close.

Rabin was killed not long afterward. Then Matt and Sara died; then the TWA tragedy occurred. The toll that this can take on a belief in God is immeasurable. When I lived in Israel, I was very happy to be living a traditional Jewish life. After I went through all these losses, even the idea of Shabbat candles broke my heart. I've never been the most rit-ually inclined person, but it felt like the rhythm of my life had left me. Jerusalem just became a memory, and another bloodstain in the news. And, just as every tragedy in Jewish history is connected with Tisha B'Av, so too all loss reminds me of Jerusalem. "When you build a house," our sages taught, "leave one wall unpainted, in memory of Jerusalem. When you put on your jewelry, leave one piece off, in memory of Jerusalem."

Acher, the third rabbi in the story, used to have a name. He was Elisha ben Abuya. But when he saw tragedy, he lost his faith, and he became known simply as "Other"—Acher. He looked, and he left his religion.

That I am still able to talk to God in whatever way I do, and serve in whatever way I do, is a gift I never take for granted. I have found ways to look, and leave, and come back. But I come back changed. In Judaism, three things change one's Hebrew name: illness, conversion, and becoming clergy. I am three for three. If I had not found ways to change my name, I would have been like Acher; I would have left my religion.

Akiva Left in Peace

I miss you, my Jerusalem, Jerusalem of gold and copper and light. My memory is darkened during the day, but my dreams are still bright. Sometimes I am there, and I remember every stone on the street and the strange blue of the sky, the taste of the food and the camaraderie, the joy and the community. So, when I enter the Pardes now, it is a virtual world, the world of my best imaginings. It is a place where the pain is integrated, balanced tightly like a tent stretched over the tent poles. It is a beautiful place. Maybe I will go back someday, so I can show my daughters how breathtaking and how wondrous it can be. But to find peace, I needed to leave. My work is not in Israel, but here.

When I was serving as a student rabbi in Colorado, I was witness to a woman dying, peacefully, of old age. Sophie died on a Friday night, just as her daughter said the blessing over the Shabbat candles at her mother's side. The only other sound was a recording of Barbara Streisand singing "Avinu Malkeinu," set on a loop. It is said that when someone dies on Shabbat, their soul leaves them with a kiss.

As a rabbi, you quickly learn the difference between a bad death and a good death, a death that comes with violence and a death that comes with a kiss. I can never bring back those I have lost. I can never undo the bad deaths. But with every dying or dead person that I care for, with everyone I accompany into the next world, this world is slightly repaired. This is what we call *tikkun*.

Sophie knew she was at the end of her life. She told me she wanted a Jewish burial, and to have her body prepared and cared for in the traditional way. She wanted to know that the end of her life would be sanctified. She asked me to promise her it would be so. Once again, I found myself making a promise I did not know if I could keep. I knew that somehow this commitment would end up with me in a cold room with a dead body, and I smelled the sea and the gasoline. But this time was different. This time, I drew a community together to make a death holy, and we pulled it off with elegance and grace.

A college town in Colorado is not New York City, when it comes to Jewish ritual supplies. We had to be creative. We went to Linens 'n' Things to buy material for the shrouds. A colleague from rabbinical school faxed me the guide to doing a *taharah*, a ritual cleaning of the body before burial. I assembled a group of women from the congregation to serve as an impromptu *chevrah kadisha*, Jewish burial society. These were women who had never done anything like this before and probably never would again. We arranged to use a room at the local, non-Jewish funeral home, where the staff was astonished to see laypeople willing to come into contact with death. There would be no embalming, no illusion that the dead person was sleeping. Years later, when my grandmother died, the conversation at the wake was about what color her lipstick should have been. She was prepared respectfully, in keeping with her own family's traditions. Still, I sat for a moment and thought of the loving ritual that we did for Sophie in Colorado. I wish something similar could have been done for my grandmother.

We followed the guide to the letter, singing as we washed each part of Sophie's body. We had a small bag of earth to put in the coffin, acquired thanks to the efforts of the funeral director. The earth was from Israel, to connect her with the Holy Land. We wrapped her in the shrouds. Then congregants took turns as *shomrim*, guardians, sitting beside the coffin so there was never a moment when Sophie was alone. The funeral was the next day, and it happened just as she wanted. I stood in the cold room and smelled the sea and the gasoline. But no one else did. We did right by Sophie, and I managed to make something good from something horrible. Now, whenever I hear "Avinu Malkeinu," I think of Jerusalem, and I think of Colorado. I think of the pain of Tisha B'Av, and the peace of Rosh Hashanah. I don't look back, and I leave in peace.

The Shabbat after Tisha B'Av is Shabbat Nachamu, the Sabbath of Comfort. It centers on a passage from Isaiah, "Comfort ye, comfort ye, my people." There is so much brokenness in this world. The best we can do is to share our stories, and begin to comfort one another.

12

Elul

Hit-or-Mitzvah

Man plans, God laughs. —Yiddish proverb

What Do Rabbis Do at Night?

"I can't imagine how deep your conversations must be at home." Occasionally, when someone finds out that both Lisa and I are rabbis, they say something along those lines. I think they imagine that our every conversation is about the Talmud, and that we never, ever laugh. They would probably be shocked and disappointed to see our nightly Scrabble games or card games, how we sit at the dining room table with popcorn or—for a special treat—a selection of interesting cheeses. We talk, and we read.

On Mondays, we read catalogues. On Tuesdays, we read *The New Yorker*. On Wednesdays, we read the local paper. On Thursdays, we read *The Onion*. On Fridays, we sleep. By the time it comes to Saturday night, we have run out of reading material.

The last Saturday night in December, we were particularly hard up. Lisa was almost eight months pregnant and was looking for distraction. It was after Christmas, so the flood of catalogues had dried up; the local paper had taken a week off, and we hadn't been in Manhattan to get *The Onion*.

The local paper taking a week off was no small disruption. Usually its material sustained us even past Wednesday nights. The same reporter writes most of the articles, which have a uniquely alarmist slant. It is the only paper I know of that can make the opening of a Starbucks sound like a pogrom. A sampling of the headlines would look something like this: Teenagers hanging out on corners! Mayor and cronies taking over schools! Buddhist principal imposing religious beliefs! How yoga poisons our children! The plight of the gifted child! Promises by local police to crack down on teens and their loitering ways! Nuclear developments in Iran—and their effect on local food prices!

Other aspects of the paper are more subtle. Sometimes Lisa and I will challenge each other to find the item that catches our attention on any particular page. One night, it was a description of how a school parent who happened to be a cardiologist brought four human hearts to a fifth-grade class. The irony is the paper's disproportionate interest in the educational system, given that, according to the 2000 U.S. census, over 40 percent of Riverdale residents are over 50 and almost 80 percent of the neighborhood's households have no children. Despite this, the children of others seem to be of interest, and their pedagogical and moral development is of great concern. And when it comes to teenagers, there is no doubt that they present a clear and present danger. The paper reports that the local community center is trying to lure them off their wayward paths by inviting them to audition for musicals, while the library has a book club for teens.

The Onion, for all its satire, falls short.

And so, on that night, Lisa and I were reduced to talking about the subtleties of microwave popcorn, which was our midnight snack. I liked the new kind we were eating, because it tasted like the sort you get in movie theaters; Lisa didn't like it, for exactly the same reason.

We don't actually get to many movies, though we watch what we can at home. It has taken awhile for us to find the places where our cultural tastes overlap. We have tried to expand each others' horizons about movies and everything else. Lisa was raised without the benefits of TV, so she has realistic views of money and sexuality—whereas I was convinced at a young age that, when the time came, I would simply win a bundle on a game show and take home the lady on top of my *new car*. If I learned anything from the hundreds of unsupervised hours I spent watching Benny Hill, it was that, if a sixty-five-year-old Englishman could get hot chicks, I could too.

When I visited Lisa in England, she took me to baroque chamber music concerts in sixteenth-century music halls. So when she came to the United States, I felt it was my duty, as an ambassador of the land of opportunity, to expose this beautiful and bewildered Canadian to the ways of my country.

The process was challenging. One night, we decided to rent a movie to drown out the sounds of roaches skittering across the floor of our Park Slope apartment. I asked her to bring back *Galaxy Quest*. She came home with *Battlefield Earth*. "I never remember the names of movies," admitted Lisa, a woman who can relate with much verve the history of the Jewish people in the Second Temple period. She doesn't just have trouble remembering titles. Plots also are elusive. She can parse a verb in biblical Hebrew or Greek, but she can't untangle the story line of *Ocean's Eleven*. I do a lot of explaining.

After many episodes of *The Simpsons* and *Buffy the Vampire Slayer*—which I convinced her she needed to watch to understand American youth—certain patterns in our tastes emerged. Lisa always falls for the good girl, and I am inevitably drawn to the bad girl. I am generally more interested in the complicated character's self-destructive torment, whereas Lisa has a soft spot for happy endings. These patterns are especially clear when we are watching a rerun of one of our favorite movies, *The Mummy Returns*. At one point in this strangely compelling archaeological thriller, the good girl and the bad girl have a fight scene involving costumes that resemble nothing so much as slave Leia's chain bikini in *Return of the Jedi*, a formative image for us both.

One afternoon, Lisa and I were sharing a cupcake on Seventy-second Street when we saw a woman leave the store who we were convinced was a character from the film. Lisa thought the woman was her favorite, the benevolent and gutsy heroine, Evie the adventurous librarian, whereas I was sure the woman was the one I fancied, the Mummy's newly resurrected consort, Anakhsenamun. We followed her for three blocks to try to catch a glimpse.

It's rare to be star-struck in New York. Ethan Hawke is everywhere, and Christiane Amanpour was holding court in the back of Sarabeth's. Lisa saw Harry from *Sex and the City* in Columbus Bakery, the day after he had been naked on HBO. As for me, I almost ran over a famous chef one day in the Village. I immediately recognized the portly man in orange clogs and a ponytail, wearing a vest and shorts, looking like an overgrown stunt double from the Hobbit. The car barely could brake, and I bounced, then squealed to a stop. On the basis of my previous experience, I had cause for concern—I still have a gun-shaped dent on the hood of my car from the time a security guard did a Steven Segal body-roll over it while chasing a shoplifter on a bicycle through the parking lot of an enormous mall in New Jersey. The only thing that made the Batali incident different was that I was afraid that, in addition to being slapped with manslaughter charges, I would be on the front page of a New York City tabloid. I could see the headline now, "Rabbi Irons Chef."

On this particular night, however, we were far removed from celebrity Italian cuisine. We only had the popcorn. We contemplated the social justice value of this particular brand, which gave part of the purchase price to charity, and we wondered whether we could claim it as a tax deduction. Little did we know that another tax deduction would be coming our way unexpectedly soon.

At this precise moment, Lisa's water broke, five weeks before her due date. Earlier that evening, her parents had joined us for dinner; they were in town to help us get ready, and we'd invited them over to have some time together that didn't involve handing them laundry or sending them out shopping. Looking back, we should have known better. When my water broke, six years earlier, it was also after a dinner party. Then too, we had cleaned the house and cooked for our guests, and to this day I am convinced that that is why my water broke the next morning, and another guest came early. Perhaps we should take the Torah more seriously when it describes how Abraham and Sarah show hospitality by feeding the angels, and then their guests surprise them by announcing Isaac's impending birth.

When my water broke, Lisa was in the shower. I spent ten minutes calling her name from the other bathroom. She jokes that it's a good thing she showered then, because she didn't have time to for the first three weeks of Ariella's life. I was less amused. But my bags were packed, and we knew that at any time, we might need to get up and go. She was due on Valentine's Day, February 14, and born on Groundhog Day, February 2. The greatest negative aspect of the timing was that Janet Jackson's infamous wardrobe malfunction had happened at the Super Bowl the day before, so all that was on the television for the long hours of labor was the coverage—or lack thereof—of her breasts.

This time, we thought we had over a month before the baby would come. We had cleaned up, Lisa's parents had come, we had eaten and they had left, and we'd cleaned up again. And then we sat down to eat popcorn, and her water broke. "Many waters cannot quench love," we read in the Song of Songs. It's true, many waters can't quench love, but they can certainly scare the hell out of you. We called Lisa's parents back to the apartment, we packed our bags, and then we went to the hospital. It was my grandmother's birthday, December 27. That would be the day that Alice was born.

Early Bird Special

The Eternal, slow to anger and abounding in kindness . . . Attribute of mercy, turn on our behalf and enter your pleas before your Creator, and ask for mercy on behalf of your people, for every heart is ailing and every head is sick.

—Piyyut by Amittai (penitential prayer from the Selichot pre–High Holy Day service)

Thirty-five weeks is an in-between time to give birth. From the moment we came in, the doctors spoke about the baby being on the cusp; there was a good chance that she would be developed enough not to have any problems, and there was also a chance she would need help.

Alice looked perfect. But she needed help. I watched her being born, and held my breath for the long moment that it took her to cry. By the time the first hour had passed, it was clear that Alice had to go to the Neonatal Intensive Care Unit, the NICU. I spent most of that first hour holding her. She grabbed my finger and looked into my eyes. I was reminded of the scene in *Dune* where a very old soul is called down into a very little body. Alice was in between worlds. She smelled like sea water, like she had just gone to the beach— and for the first time, I smelled that salty smell and did not have a flashback. I was simply there with her. I welcomed her to the world, to her own wonderland, and told her that we weren't sure how far the rabbit hole would go, but that we knew she would be in good hands. I wanted to just keep her and run away, but we could see that she couldn't hold enough oxygen by herself, and that she was fading. Even the pediatrician said it was hard to take her to the NICU, but we knew that was where she needed to be. I let her out of my arms.

It would be the last time I would hold her, for almost a week. Alice went from looking like a normal baby to being some miniature semblance of Darth Vader, less human and more machine. She was hooked up to an apparatus for breathing and to an IV. Her eyes were covered to protect her against the lights. Her nose and mouth were covered by tubes. Her arms and feet had sensors and IVs and, very soon, bandages to cover the many places from which the nurses took blood. There was more apparatus than there was baby, though she kicked off everything she could. For that first week, we spent a lot of time talking about her toes: how expressive they were, and whether each day they were a little less blue. Mostly, though, it was because we could see so little of her face. And whenever we touched her through the incubator portholes, it would send her vital signs plummeting.

The first two nights, after Lisa was asleep two floors down, I went up and sat beside Alice. I felt camouflaged, sitting quietly and watching my baby. I started to learn her patterns: which cry she made when she wet her diaper, and which when she was upset. I watched the monitors and listened to the rhythm of the machines. Sitting there, I thought about how glad I was to be Jewish, that I didn't have to find someone to baptize her and ensure the safety of her soul. I knew her soul was good, and that she herself needed to decide to stay. She was just as confused as any of us by her early entry into the world.

I also thought about the *akedah*, when Abraham almost sacrifices his son. When you go to the NICU, you need to be willing to give over your child and hope it's for the good. You take this tiny human being whom you have cared for, for months upon months, this child whom you have dreamed of for years, and you let her be poked and prodded and isolated and restrained. Nurses could inspire waves of gratitude if they were kind, and helpless fury if they were rough. The change of the number on a monitor, the whispering of the word "intubation," an urgent beeping from the machine, which the nurses knew to screen out but which to a parent was potential disaster: all these things became my world.

We signed up for what Lisa called the pessimist's parking pass, which gave us parking privileges for a month. It involved taking a letter to the parking office at the hospital lot, introducing us as a family with a child in intensive care. We felt we were joining an undesirable club. We got parent passes from a security guard, who was almost too busy chatting with her friends to take our photos, and we felt a new kind of anger. We went home without our baby. Lisa said she felt as if she had a phantom limb; she kept feeling Alice moving inside her.

The day that we could hold her, the day that we could see her face, was a day I will never forget. I cradled her and I told her how the littlest people carry the greatest responsibility, and short people like her mother run the world. I told her she came from a good line of strong, small people. I looked again into her eyes, and hoped with all my heart that she too would grow strong. I thought of the words from the Jewish baby-naming ceremony, "May this little one become big."

Standing there in the NICU, I remembered all the times people had told us to have faith. When we went through three years of infertility, the doctors said, "You're people of faith. Have faith." When one of our pregnancies showed bad signs early on, the doctors said, "You're people of faith. Have faith." That pregnancy ended in a miscarriage. When something looked wrong on a late ultrasound in this pregnancy, the doctors said, "You're people of faith. Have faith." In those moments and at this moment, both Lisa and I realized: for us, that's not what faith is all about.

We see enough tragedies in our work to know that bad things happen. Not only that, but bad things happen to good people, and on a regular basis. We had no illusions about things that could go wrong, and we had no delusions that for some reason we would be exempt. We could not comfort each other with platitudes. Faith could not mean that we knew things would be fine. Rather, we would work with a model of controlled chaos. Faith is not about results; it is about putting one foot in front of the other, and facing whatever may come. *Uvecharta b'chayim*, we read in the Torah on Yom Kippur: "You shall choose life." I have always understood that to mean: choose to live the life that you are in. Rarely is there a simple choice between life and death. Rather, the choice is how best to live in the grey: how to help a newly born human being choose to stay in this world, and how to make that choice, oneself, day after difficult day.

There is a certain camaraderie in the NICU, much more than in the infertility clinic. In both places, though, there is a default community; everyone is in the midst of her or his own story, but there is an acknowledgment that we are all in the same boat. In these situations, no one ever gave us a hard time for being gay. The pain of infertility, the anxiety in the NICU—like the broadest definition of diversity, none of these experiences discriminate on the basis of sexuality or religion. Hatred so often hides behind anonymity, but in the NICU there is a rawness that makes this almost impossible. You look across the room and see a Muslim woman in a hijab or a Chasidic man or a lesbian couple and you think only: I hope their kid is okay. I hope all our kids are okay.

When we go to the NICU as rabbis, it is rarely for a situation that is good. I have always been impressed by the doctors and nurses who work there, how adept they are, and how they find a graceful way to inhabit this twilight zone of babies who are born too soon. As parents, we were awed by how they were able to navigate this difficult terrain, to make the days a little shorter and the nights a little gentler. In the end, Alice was there for just over a week.

Call of Doody: Very Special-Ops

And they shall beat their swords into plowshares, and their spears
into pruning hooks.   —Isaiah 2:4

We got ready to bring Alice home. For months,
Ariella had been making her own preparations. "When the
sac breaks, the bells go on," she would say—meaning, when
Lisa's water broke, Ariella's job was to put collars with bells
on the cats, so we could keep track of them. Ever attuned to
any domestic disruption, the cats were prescribed anti-
anxiety medication when Ariella was born, and we had
them ready this time as well.

That was the extent of our low-tech preparation. There
was high-tech preparation, too. The challenge was to be
able to check on the children, especially once they would
be sharing a room. The baby books are filled with descrip-
tions of how problematic baby monitors can be. Either all
the wireless devices in a home interfere with one another,
leaving you with no clear signal, or the signal is too clear
and you end up listening to your neighbor's baby—or
phone conversations, as we once discovered. There is both
humor and comfort in listening to your neighbors' inter-
actions with their parents, but at it's hard to get around
the fact that it's a gross invasion of privacy (not to mention that they could probably hear our conversations, as
well).

Thinking outside the box, I realized that night-vision
goggles could be a solution. How better to see the children
at night without waking them up? However, a problem
remained: some things are just not on the registry. I turned
to my brother for advice—and military gear. A new video
game, *Call of Duty*, had just been released; the premium
edition included a pair of night vision goggles, which he just
happened to have. I explained the situation, and he gener-
ously agreed to lend them to us.

The goggles are evocative of the scene at the end of *Silence of the Lambs*, where the killer stalks the intrepid young FBI agent, played by Jodie Foster, in the darkness of his basement. It is one of the most suspenseful moments in modern film. Only by virtue of her cat-quick reflexes does she hear the click of his gun before he shoots, and, despite his night-vision advantage, manage to kill him and save the day. One day, when our daughters see this movie, I hope it brings to mind warm and fuzzy memories of childhood, rather than terror. May they know that we were always vigilant, even in the face of complete darkness. Or maybe they will just think we were crazy.

How to cope with adversity is a perennial question. For some people, the solution may be to pretend nothing had ever happened. For others, it's to be paranoid every time their child sneezes. Others of us turn to infrared devices.

Alice will never remember how sick she was, but for us it will always be the beginning of the story. We are left with the image of her face covered with tubes through the first week of her life, and the memory of Ariella crying when her little sister couldn't come home. We are grateful that what happened was not worse, and we are grateful it was not longer. We are grateful that our biggest challenge now is to treat her as if she had always been well, while keeping vigilant against harm. In the face of controlled chaos, we have to make life go on as normal. But we stay frosty.

Elul, the month leading up to Rosh Hashanah, reminds us to live our lives well. It is a month of introspection and preparation, and also a month that celebrates love—love between us and God, and love between human beings. Love is disruptive. It opens us up to controlled chaos, to vulnerability, to loss. As a child, I never imagined that I would get married, or that I would become a parent. Now that all of this has come to pass, life seems at once more beautiful and more fragile.

Lisa and I got married a month after 9/11. Some of our friends and relatives could not come because of new limitations on travel, and, for most who were invited, it was the first celebration they would be part of since that cataclysmic day. We thought briefly about rescheduling. And then I realized: there is no better way to counter terrorism than to have a big gay Jewish wedding in the heart of New York City. So we did. It was a great gathering. People came from across the Jewish denominations, and across faiths. Our parents met for the first time the week before. My father smoked his pipe on the steps of the synagogue, beside a major Jewish theologian, who also had a pipe in his hand. Rabbi Al was the officiant, and his voice, along with that of our friend Cantor Rica Timman, filled the room with hope. There is a Jewish concept called *hiddur mitzvah*, which entails taking something that is required and making it beautiful. For example, on Shabbat one requirement is to make a blessing over wine; a way of making this beautiful would be to make sure that the Kiddush cup is beautiful and that the wine is good. We are required to face what comes our way. How we do so is in our hands.

I believe our task is to make the best of any situation, to try and find humor and creativity and grace. This can be hard to do when you are watching someone you love being stitched up, or letting your child be taken from your arms. But we still aspire to elegant solutions to practical problems—that's where the night-vision goggles come in. May this little one become big, and may we be privileged to watch her grow.

13

Purim Katan

Customs and Gratuities Included

He who is glad of heart, feasts constantly.
—Proverbs 15:15

I love you. This is what family does.
—Sally Bellafiore

After my grandfather died, my grandmother stopped going out, and she stopped answering her phone. Callers couldn't even leave a message; she had never had an answering machine, and she was not about to get one. She saw it as one piece of modern technology that she would never be able to wrap her head around. "Who am I and where the hell am I going? If someone needs to reach me, they know where I am." Sometimes, I would be upstairs with her, and the phone would ring. "Grandma," I would ask, "why don't you answer it?" "I just don't feel like talking right now," she would say.

Late one night, her phone rang. Surprised by the hour and thinking this must be an emergency, she took the call—only to hear two teenage boys laughing on the other end of the line. They were making prank calls. Realizing that they had reached an old woman, they decided to harass her: "This is the pharmacy, ma'am. We have your order of a thousand condoms ready. Where do you want us to deliver them?" She paused and then answered, "Oh dear. I'm an eighty-year-old widow. What do I need a thousand condoms for? One or two, maybe, but not a thousand!" Flustered, the teenagers hung up, and never bothered her again. The next morning, she came downstairs with a smile we hadn't seen in years. She had bested the young, and she was back. Her sense of humor had returned.

When I came home from Israel, my grandmother would get her social security check each month and take me out to Vincent's Clam Bar, a local Italian restaurant. She would get spaghetti with white wine and clam sauce, and I would get anything that had neither clams nor wine. For a long time, Vincent's only hired waiters who were tall, dark, and handsome—and male. Eventually, women broke through the red-sauce ceiling. But when my grandmother and I had our lunches, she requested only her favorite male waiters. She considered it part of dessert to flirt with them. At the bank, she would get a few crisp bills, perfect for folding and slipping into the waiters' pockets: "Here's a little something for you, honey buns."

This made me very uncomfortable, and she seemed to enjoy my discomfort even more than her dessert. But I never wanted our lunches to end. I remembered the days after my grandfather died, when she wouldn't pick up the phone, much less go out to eat. And so I saw these meals as a victory. We made our own private holiday, celebrating her return to herself.

According to the Jewish calendar, each year contains twelve months, based on the lunar cycle. To keep the festivals consistent with the seasons set by the sun, an entire leap-month is inserted, and this thirteenth month is included seven times over the course of nineteen years. This leap-month is always the month of Adar, the month in which Purim falls. The question then arises: in which Adar, the first or the second, is Purim celebrated? The answer is that Purim is celebrated in the second month of Adar but some still mark it in the first month as well, by eating a festive meal. This small celebration is known as "Purim Katan," "the Little Purim."

Over time, Purim Katan developed independently from its original connection to the calendar and even from the specific connection to the Purim story. It became a matter of local custom, a holiday that any family or community could establish at any time to express gratitude for deliverance from a threat. In this way, individual Jewish communities put their own holidays on the calendar. Some celebrated surviving earthquakes and other natural disasters, and others commemorated weathering blood libels and persecutions. Even individual families would proclaim certain days as Purim Katan, on the basis of something good that happened to them. The point is simply this: when we escape adversity, we celebrate. And when we celebrate, we feast. For me and my grandmother, each of those trips to Vincent's was a Purim Katan, a commemoration of her escape from depression.

My grandmother emerged from her depression, but her final years were fraught with dementia. Still, glimmers of her former self were visible. At my ordination, the sound system in the sanctuary was deafening. The feedback and volume gave the ceremony a decidedly purple haze. In the middle of a piece being sung by a new cantor, my grandmother stood up, threw her hearing aid down, and yelled out, "Would someone please shut her the hell up?" Those who didn't know my grandmother buzzed about the senile old lady doing the screaming. Those of us who knew her better understood this was vintage Sally shining through. She had always loved opera and the vocal arts, but she had no patience for a bad sound system.

My grandmother's final holiday meal in our home was a Thanksgiving dinner. She fell asleep in her seat, but not before eating half the mozzarella balls on the table. The other half fell under her chair. Miller swarmed around her feet, catching the scraps. We all knew this would be her last Thanksgiving. As difficult as it was to watch my mother and aunt struggle to feed her with dignity, we were grateful to be together with her at the table one last time. By week's end, she was gone.

My family asked me to officiate at her funeral. It never occurred to anyone that a rabbi might be uncomfortable doing a funeral for her Catholic-turned-Baptist-turned-agnostic grandmother, and it never occurred to me to turn down an opportunity to honor her. I found a Presbyterian minister with whom I could co-officiate, in an attempt to make the service meaningful for the Christians in attendance—which, of course, was everyone but me, Lisa, and my aunt's Jewish husband.

I was seven months pregnant with Ariella at the funeral. I had so much wanted my grandmother to meet her. Lisa and I gave Ariella the middle name Rose, in honor of my grandmother's formal name, Rosaria. Both of our daughters are named for our grandmothers: Ariella for my Grandma, Alice for Lisa's Bubbie.

Both of our grandmothers were known by the name Sally. Like many immigrants of their generation, they and their husbands took generic names that obscured their ethnicity. They were two women from very different backgrounds: my Grandma Sally came from a family of Italian Catholic missionaries in Tunis, and Lisa's Bubbie Sally came from a shtetl in the Ukraine. They never knew each other in life. But they are brought together through these two little girls of a generation they will never know.

Lisa and I only hope that our daughters have the gift of our grandmothers' strength. Both women knew that times could be tough, and that when times were good, it was worth celebrating. Their respective tables were piled high with very different foods, but they shared a conviction that having everyone at the table was in itself worth celebrating. Each meal was a Purim Katan.

The *Shulchan Aruch*, the great sixteenth-century code of Jewish law, literally means "the set table," and its most important commentary is known as "the tablecloth," *hamapah*. The commentator, Rabbi Moses Isserles, can be seen as an early pluralist. He helped make the *Shulchan Aruch* a source that everyone could use. Its original author, Joseph Caro, wrote from a Sephardic perspective, but Isserles added an Ashkenazic gloss so that Caro's work could be used by Jews who followed either tradition. Isserles's tablecloth let everyone sit together at Caro's table.

In writing about Purim Katan, Isserles notes that some Jews feast in the first month of Adar, while others do not. He presents a compromise position: you should just eat more than usual. Our grandmothers would have approved. Then, Isserles provides a final quote, "He who is glad of heart, feasts constantly" (Proverbs 15:15). It would make more sense the other way around: the one who feasts constantly is glad of heart. But that is not what the Bible says, and that is not what Isserles is using the verse to teach. Rather, it is when we consciously orient our hearts to be glad, that we come together at the table and are able to feast. Like that chicken in the shuk in Jerusalem, we are looking for a way to survive, and thrive, on our own terms.

When my grandmother moved into the nursing home at the very end of her life, my parents gave me and Lisa the bedroom furniture that my grandparents had received as a wedding gift. It is a beautiful set done in heavy mahogany. One of the pieces is a small desk. It was originally intended as a vanity, but my grandfather used it to store his stationery supplies and his knives. Recently, I discovered a thin yellowed stack of papers in the desk. For reasons that will forever remain unknown, he had taped them underneath the large middle drawer. Upon inspection, I instantly recognized the faded brown type on crisp ivory paper riddled with grease stains. The papers were menus from Beefsteak Charlie's, cut on the edges with my grandfather's trademark pinking shears.

My mind flashed back to Beefsteak Charlie's, the restaurant where my family would go to celebrate everyone's collective birthdays once a year. Most of the adults in the family were born between Thanksgiving and New Year's, so we would go out together and celebrate them all at once. In the days before televised competitive eating, this was a sight to behold. Beefsteak Charlie's was known for its all-you-can-eat salad bar—and also for the rule that customers had to place their orders before leaving the table to avail themselves of the buffet. We would wait for the waiter, wait for everyone to order, and then bolt up from our seats to race to the salad bar. The main attraction was the fresh bowl of shrimp. We would simultaneously grab the tongs and hunt for the crustaceans in the ice, as if they were buried treasure. A successful hunt resulted in plates loaded to maximum height, like personal pink ziggurats. My grandfather was the only one who wouldn't go to the buffet; instead, he ordered a side salad with his dinner and sat smiling while everyone around him jumped up for the salad bar. I always thought he was amused by the frenzy.

Now I stood at my grandfather's desk, decades after his death, holding these menus that he must have taken when no one was looking, probably when we were all chasing the shrimp and he was left alone. Written on the menus, in his distinctive script, were the dates of family birthdays that we had celebrated there together. He must have sat down at his desk and written the names and dates when he got home. It was a sentimental side of him that I had never before seen.

I looked at the names of the members of my family and thought of all their stories. Then I thought of the family I have formed, and the way we have filled these same desk drawers: the address labels, with Lisa's name and mine side by side; the programs from our wedding; the stationary with Ariella's and Alice's names; cards from my mother, in her beautiful script; and the spare *Rabbi's Manual*, which we keep there just in case.

There is no room for this little desk in our bedroom, so we keep it in the dining room. It has witnessed our own sacred moments. Rosh Hashanah, when we use the honey jar and apple dish painted with our children's tiny feet. Passover, when we invite congregants, conversion students, family, and friends to our seder to share their journeys. The night we were eating popcorn when Lisa's water broke, and Alice entered our lives. Each of these moments is a Purim Katan. Old stories and new beginnings, integration and transformation. Whatever differences we bring to the table, the labels fade when they are reflected in the faces of the ones we love. The stories take center stage. This is what family does.

About the Author

Rabbi Andrea Myers has shared her unique stories around the world. After receiving her B.A. in neuroscience from Brandeis University, she studied for two years in Jerusalem and was ordained at the Academy for Jewish Religion (AJR), an interdenominational seminary in New York City. She has been part of the faculty and administration of AJR and has served as the co-president of its professional alumni organization, the Association of Rabbis and Cantors. Rabbi Myers is a member of the New York Board of Rabbis. She currently lives in New York City, and has led congregations from the Rocky Mountains to the Borscht Belt.